For Anyone who has ever h
find one, Wheel of Wisdom ... ... *y* ....
energies of your inner turtle and hare to give your
dream a plan and put a great plan behind your
dream.

    Your inner hare is the visionary who spins
out a dream; your inner turtle is the planner who
grounds the dream and takes it forward, one step
at a time. Turtle teaches focus, discipline, patience
and helps you align the plan to the dream. Hare
teaches courage, thinking in possibilities, creative
imagination and helps you let go in order to seed
a new dream.

    The Wheel of Wisdom is a progressive cycle of
self-enquiry in which you ask yourself the right
questions about your wishes, fantasies and goals.

    Each time we follow a dream our inner turtle
and hare embark on a journey. Step on the Wheel
of Wisdom to discover your innate "owl wisdom"
and true dream potential.

For Susan,
A soul-sister on
the dream journey.
Embrace your visions!

April.

That holy dream, that holy dream,
While all the world were chiding,
Hath cheered me as a lovely beam,
A lonely spirit guiding.
EDGAR ALLEN POE

Previous Publications:

Mad about Muffins, Clarke Irwin, 1982
Mad about Cheddar, Irwin, 1983
Fun in the Kitchen, Irwin, 1984
Wild about Muffins, Barrons (U.S.), 1985
Love in the Blended Family, NC Press, 1988

THE WHEEL OF WISDOM

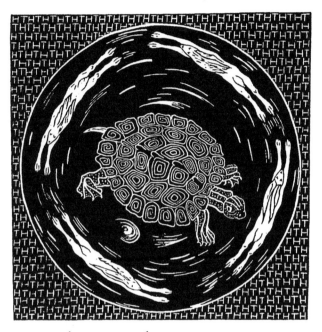

A Turtle and Hare Journey
to your Dream

ANGELIKA CLUBB

NC Press Limited

Toronto, 1994

Illustrations by Janet Stahle-Fraser, M.A.
  Tapawingo Studio, Baysville, Ontario, Canada
Photograph of Angelika Clubb by Audrey van Petegem
Cover Design by Gerry Ginsberg

Canadian Cataloguing in Publication Data

Main Entry under title:
Wheel of Wisdom
ISBN 1-55021-082-3
1. China – Social conditions.   2. Taiwan – Social
conditions.   3. Hong Kong – Social conditions.
I. Title.
DS779.23.P87 1993   951.05'9   C93-095258-8

We would like to thank the Ontario Arts Council, the Ontario Publishing
Centre, the Ontario Ministry of Culture, Tourism and Recreation, the
Ontario Development Corporation, the Canada Council and the Government
of Canada, Department of Canadian Heritage and the Association for the
Export of Canadian Books for their assistance in the production and marketing of
this book.

New Canada Publications, a division of NC Press Limited,
Box 452, Station A, Toronto, Ontario, Canada, M5W 1H8.

Printed and bound in Canada

CONTENTS

Acknowledgments

My deep gratitude and love to:

David Clubb, my partner in the dream and the plan.

Rose and Kurt Neumann, my first turtle and hare teachers, whose support at a most crucial time made all the difference.

Evelyn Reid, a wise turtle who first coined the phrase "every dream needs a plan" and in whose kitchen I received wonderful feedback.

Kurt and Lu Schick, whose friendship, insight and professional input were indispensable to the book's development.

Marie Stilkind, who first tackled the manuscript, contributing her creativity, editing expertise and intuition.

Cristian and Karen Koos, Heidi Neumann-Hill, Maria Casimirri, Elaine and Yvonne Pitre, Kit and Carl Ljungberg, Patricia Harris, Elizabeth Tudhope, Artemus Cole, Jeanette Metler, Brian Williams, Sonya Sullivan, Ruth Bernold, Steve O'Neill, Terri Richard, Judy Fulton, Janet Parker-Vaughan, Christine Hodson, Adrian Doubleday, Jack McClelland and Linda Quirino, Donna and Jim Drury, Heather and Jean Kingshott and Sara Thiereault, for all they have individually contributed.

Brenda and Dave Richards, who designed and constructed my special writing space and unknowingly created a "wish wall." And Emil and Irene Shamash who provided the desk and the chair so that I might begin.

Lynette Brooker of *Circling Hawk Center* and *Country Clutter*, who generously shared her wisdom, friendship and her contacts when I launched *Angelika & Co.*; Jim Maguire of *The Book Store*, and Sylvia Purdon, who supported it from the start; Frances Cowan, Geila Bar-David and Terry and Sandy Cowan, who filled the space with prayers and music the night before I opened; and the many wonderful year-round and summer customers who have made my store more than its gifts.

Audrey van Petegem, for contributing the backcover photo.

Janet Stahle-Fraser, whose friendship, vision for the cover, and commitment to this book inspired my *inner turtle* to see it through to press.

Publisher, Caroline Walker, Janet Walker, Wanita Storms and Gim-yu Eng at NC Press for believing in the book, their enthusiasm, and for pulling it together in hare time.

All the men and women in my circle, as well as our children, Amy, Christopher, Andrew and Kate Clubb for what they have taught me about love.

Introduction

I had gone away for the week-end with my friend Evelyn to her lakeside cottage. Both of us were in somewhat of a "limbo space": Evelyn was between contracts, and I between writing projects. Among other things we were eager to talk about future ideas, perhaps even come up with a plan.

Evelyn, a down-to-earth businesswoman, brought with her some "essentials": bathroom caulking (she always completed one small but concrete task per day), a light novel and a good current newspaper. I also brought my essentials: my journal and favourite pen, music and mediation cassettes, and a good lemon loaf. And so we two had a wonderful time together, sharing the dreams and plans of our respective worlds, the world of the dreamer and the world of the planner.

My partner David's personal dream had taken us to the north woods of Muskoka, Canada, a move away from family, community connections, city and a known lifestyle. As each family member adjusted to the changes in their own way, I began a period of retreat and self-enquiry to reexamine my own goals. I began to explore former dreams and the motivation behind those desires in an effort to understand my own dream journey.

I also asked myself some elemental questions: Why had some of my dreams simply "worked" while others, despite my best intentions, had spun into frustrating cycles of incomplete projects and unrealized plans? One key seemed to be that I did not know how to fully engage in a step-by-step process which included a strong plan along with what I perceived as "turtle discipline." The well-known fable, *The Tortoise and the Hare* became my metaphor.

Dreamers and planners basically express two distinct and contrasting personality types, they are primarily turtles or hares. This book is about rescripting an old fable and an old attitude. If dreamers and planners could but acquire "owl wisdom" (the combination of hare creativity and turtle perserverance), then dreamers could also create great plans, and planners could engage in dreams. There are wise turtles and hares who already know how to do both. I was not one of these.

Wheel of Wisdom is about tapping into the energies of both your inner turtle and hare, giving your dream a plan, and your plan a dream, thereby achieving the potential to fulfill the goals you hope for in your life. Use the Wisdom Chapters in whatever way or order works best. Whether you are in the midst of your dream or have been drawn to read this book because you feel empty of any dream at all, you will find that no matter the stage, once you decide and begin it, the journey *is* the dream. I guarantee it will create challenge, personal growth and magic.

The dream calls to us from the rainbow's end; but the plan and the journey always begin today in the here and now. And because each day is a new possibility, a new opportunity, you can if you choose, let the dream in and begin the plan.

I wish you an unforgettable journey!

PROLOGUE

The Turtle and the Hare

A Fable Retold

A wise old owl sat on an oak,
The more he saw, the less he spoke;
The less he spoke, the more he heard;
Why aren't we like that wise old bird?
EDWARD HERSEY RICHARDS

The Turtle and the Hare

A Fable Retold

On a country road at midday, the hare and the turtle saw each other coming in the distance.

"What a dull and slow creature the turtle is," thought the hare. He scorned turtle's short thick legs, hooked toes and small head. "How ridiculously squatty and flat he looks! I wonder how he gets anywhere at all with his plodding."

Turtle, moving slowly towards Hare saw there was no way to avoid this chance encounter. "What a boastful bag of wind, Hare is," thought Turtle. "Just look at those long, gangly legs and silly ears. I wonder how he ever gets anywhere, bounding about in five directions at once." It was clear to both, as they approached one another, that no love was lost between them.

"Good-day," said the turtle formally.

"Howdy," replied the hare, "And where are you heading?"

"I'm on my way over the hill to the village," answered Turtle.

Hare could not resist. "Do you think you'll arrive there this week?" he asked.

Turtle was irritated, but dug his thick feet more firmly into the ground and continued walking. "What control I have!" he thought proudly. "That nervous ball of fur doesn't deserve an answer."

The hare was furious. To be ignored by this slow plodder was the ultimate insult!

"Good that you don't stop, you dull turtle, for I could run circles around you and the village before you could even reach the hill." Grinning, he added, "And with your short little legs, I dare say you'll never get anywhere in this life!"

Not able to contain himself any longer, Turtle raised his head from the ground and looked angrily at Hare, "I am tired of your arrogance. I have often watched you, and I am tired of how you dance around and do nothing. I accept your challenge, and we will see who arrives at the village first!"

The hare laughed, wondering how this squatty creature dared to challenge him. "I see that your head is as thick as your shell," he retorted. "I'll be waiting for you at the village gates, if you ever get there." And with one long jump, he was off, leaving the turtle far behind in a flurry of dust.

Turtle gave a deep sigh and went about his task calmly. "I know that Hare too well," he thought. "He'll be distracted by the first patch of wild greens near the path, or he'll run into an old friend and talk for hours, perhaps even change his mind altogether. No matter, I have to get there the most efficient way I know. I've been on this path many times before."

Turtle moved along with determination, looking neither to the right or left of the path. "If I stay at this pace, and stick to it without breaks, I should reach the village in time for tea." With his goal firmly in sight, he contemplated the tasty raisin biscuit he would eat when he got to the village.

In the meantime, Hare, despite his quick tongue, was in his heart of hearts a warm and generous fellow, and was already chastising himself for goading Turtle to race with him. "I think I'll invite my old friend for some ice tea after I win, and just to show there are no hard feelings, I'll buy him one of those raisin biscuits."

So preoccupied was he with Turtle, and so pleased was he with himself and his idea, he had not noticed how exhausted he suddenly felt, having sprinted up the hill at top speed. "I must remind myself to exercise more regularly," he panted. "I must rest for a bit and recover my energy, perhaps look for a bite before I go on."

In no time at all, the fast-footed hare had found himself a delicious leafy morsel just off the path, and was soon sitting to enjoy it in the cool shade of an oak tree. "Ah, this is heaven," he sighed, as he sank back on a soft cluster of moss. "I've run very hard, and I deserve this little rest. Besides, it will be hours before Turtle gets here."

The breeze felt divine. "It's so nice not to have to rush so. If I could only know how Turtle has the energy to keep going like that." And although the hare would never admit it to anyone he sometimes envied Turtle; the way he could keep going once he had made up his mind, the way Turtle was always so disciplined. And having run his fastest to gain a head start and having stuffed himself with his snack, Hare soon fell asleep. Unaware even of Owl, who sat motionless high up in the oak tree, eyes half closed, waiting in silence for Turtle.

By and by, Turtle lumbered along exactly as planned. And although the turtle would never admit it to anyone, it had been a tiresome journey so far with no rest or food. He sometimes envied Hare for his speed and bursts of enthusiasm. Hare often had great luck and great ideas. Turtle wondered how his life might be if it were as exciting as Hare's.

"Just look at you sleeping," he said to Hare under his breath as he approached the tree. "Didn't I just know something would keep you back, you silly fool. You don't think, you don't plan, and now I'm going to walk right by you and reach the village first."

Slowly and very quietly, Turtle passed the oak, unaware that Owl was watching from his high branch as he continued his journey.

The afternoon grew cool, the patch of moss felt damp and the hare awoke with a start. "Oh my! Oh my gads! Where am I?" And looking around, he remembered the turtle and the race. "What time is it? How long have I slept?" And with a jerk he bounded up leaping toward the hill to catch up and pass Turtle. "He can't possibly be there yet. It's just not possible!"

But while Hare had reached the top of the hill in a flash, he was dismayed to see in the distance Turtle approaching the village gates. Hare's marvelous jack-rabbit legs could not get him there in time, even if he could spring over rocks with gigantic leaps. "Oh, well," he thought regretfully, "Turtle has won the race after all." And for the first time, Hare noticed Owl sitting on the village gate, watching. "Darn, and a witness, too!"

Meanwhile, Turtle saw Hare coming. It was good to have won, but not altogether as satisfying as he had expected. Turtle was tired and low in spirits. How he would have enjoyed the mossy patch under the tree, and how he had wished for a little snack and a companion along the way. It had been a plodding journey after all.

With a meek smile, Hare arrived at the gate. "I know. I know. Don't say it. Slow but sure gets you there every time, right?" And remembering his good intentions, he invited Turtle for tea and biscuits.

The turtle was pleased, though it was not his way to show it. Instead, he asked Hare, "How do you think of all your ideas?"

"I let them come into my mind," answered Hare, "and then I play with them like a game to see where they want to take me."

"Sounds risky to me," replied Turtle "That's why I don't let myself get carried away."

"Too bad!" said Hare, "I scheme great dreams. Sometimes they work out, sometimes they don't." Then he laughed. "Never could figure out why some of my best ideas haven't."

"Probably because you didn't have a plan," Turtle answered wryly. "First you need a plan, then you need to stick to the plan."

"But how do you discipline yourself so well?" Hare moaned. "I used to give myself a small task every day when I first started," replied Turtle, "But you have to really want discipline or it doesn't work."

"Well I had this notion to do a cross-country journey," continued Hare eagerly, "But I wonder if I could make it. If only I had some of that enduring energy you have, Turtle!"

"That's something I could teach you easily enough," Turtle answered. "But a journey cross-country, that's too grand a dream for me."

"Not with a plan," Hare shot back. "Isn't that what you said? First you need a plan. I've got the dream, and you've got the plan, right?"

Neither Turtle nor Hare said a word for several moments. And Owl, still perched on the village gate, eyes half closed, silently watched as the pair, talking animatedly, disappeared into the village cafe.

Moral: *Turtles and hares have much to learn from one another. But owls know that* **every great dream needs a plan, every great plan, a dream.**

PART 1

The Wish Wall

Dreams are among our most precious possessions.
We hold that dreams are not just for the night alone, but they
are the stuff of daylight, outreachings of a better self, of a
better tomorrow.
ALGERNON BLACK

The Wish Wall

My office came about as the result of a special kind of timing and some extraordinary wishes.

I had done some soul searching as to whether being a working writer was really my dream after all. If I chose to live the writer's life, then it was time to leave behind kitchen-corner and dining-room-table writing, recommit to my craft and give myself space for it. I was also clear on one other thing. Creativity aside, it was now necessary to conduct my writing as a business. That was the plan.

Dave, the contracter, designed a compact space for me just off the dining room. My office would become an extension of the side porch with large windows and a soundproof door. Soon foundation blocks were placed below ground level. Enthusiastic about the progress, I hovered over Dave, chatting. Just finishing his coffee, he stuffed his paper cup into the concrete cavity in a cement block.

"Why did you stuff that in the block?" I asked.

"It's just a paper coffee cup," he answered, giving me that writers-are-strange look. "The cement is going to go over it anyway."

"But this is my sacred writing space, my new office!" I protested. "This is where the book is going to happen. If anything is going to go into the brick wall, it should be my wishes and dreams."

I removed the cup, and found a piece of paper on which I wrote the things I hoped and wished for in my life. I then scrolled it, tied a blue ribbon around it and dropped it three feet deep. The paper disappeared down the grey foundation of my wish wall in a reverent moment of silence.

"You see, there are fountains and wishing wells for wishing, but now I have a wishing wall. Why don't you put a wish in too, Dave?"

"Maybe tomorrow," he said, smiling.

But the next day it rained, and Dave couldn't mix cement. My wish wall, however, was protected and the open blocks called out for wishes. I began to write little scrolls for my friends and family. Soon I had written wishes for health, world peace, prosperity, blessings and love for those people dear to me. My friend Elizabeth instructed me on the telephone, "Just write, *For Elizabeth, the silent wish* on the note, put it in and the next time I come, I'll stand in front of your wall and make the wish myself." Clever idea, I thought.

I asked my daughter Kate, "Are you going to write your wishes and put them in my wall? This is a very special wall." Kate busied herself with dreams and wishes. The magic was contagious. Our friends across the way came with their two children to plant their wishes in my wall. The following weekend when my parents came, the wall was still open.

"This is your chance," I said. "It's time to put your dreams in my wall."

"Oh," sighed my mother, "I don't have any more dreams. I just want my girls to be happy."

"Then write that," I told her. "But I'm sure you'll think of something else as well."

My father in the meantime had placed himself in the corner of my sunporch and was thoughtfully writing.

"Oh Angie!" my mother laughed, "Only *you* would have a wish wall!" It had taken a little prodding, but my turtle mother had stretched herself and written her personal dreams on a small piece of paper. And it was good to see her having fun with it.

In a family ritual, which my father captured on video, we all watched our wishes fall deep into the wish wall.

The best wish story of all, however, was when my young friend Sara, age seven, came with her family for the evening. I explained about the many secret wishes already in the wish wall, and that we could all drop our wishes in later, in the moonlight. Immediately enchanted by the idea and with pencil and paper in hand, Sara disappeared.

"Angie, how do you spell *dog*?" she called from inside. A few minutes passed. "And how do you spell *turtle*?"

We decided to light a candle and have our son, Christopher, accompany our party with his guitar. Sara asked if she could hold the candle. In a small procession, with our rolled up wishes, young Sara led the way holding a candle in the moonlight while Christopher walked behind her, playing blues-style, *Got a Dog and his Name was Blue* on his classical guitar. It was an exquisite summer's night, the grass wet with dew, and I sang along to the tune as we walked towards the wishing wall:

> Got a wish and we're walking to the wall;
> Dropping our dreams in one and all.

Sara believed in my wall more than anyone else. And because she wanted to believe so much, she also needed to question the magic.

"Will the wish come true for sure?" she asked me. "Will it really come true if I put it in your wish wall?" When a child has trust like that, whether in a wish wall or the words of a grown-up, the responsibility feels immense.

I answered, "Sara, I'm not sure if your wish will come true, only God can know that. But I can tell you this for sure: If the wishes you are wishing today don't come true, something else will come true in its place that will be just as good, maybe even better. And you will need to be patient until that happens. And when that something better happens, you will know that it was meant for you because you wished a wish some time ago here in the wish wall."

"Okay," Sara said. And I could see that she was completely satisfied with my answer.

Adults are so much more skeptical, even when they dare to make wishes. But with Sara's wishes in my wall, how could I not believe in it? I knew, too, that whenever I became discouraged in my writing, I would have the energy of all those wonderful wishes and dreams to inspire mine.

The following Monday, Dave came to mix cement. There were almost three hundred wishes in my wall.

PART 2

Turtles and Hares as Dreamers and Planners

Behold the turtle.
He makes progress only when he sticks his neck out.
JAMES BRYANT CONANT

Turtles and Hares as Personality Types

All the thoughts of a turtle are turtles,
and of a rabbit, rabbits.
RALPH WALDO EMERSON

To be a *Turtle Type* or a *Hare Type* means expressing the positive and negative qualities we symbolically associate with turtles and hares. This means that we can express both the best of hare and turtle energy or the worst.

Often we are turtles in one area of life and hares in another. For example, you may need to function as a turtle at work, but express your hare-self when you vacation by seeking out-of-the-ordinary adventure tours. Or you may appear to be a turtle in your desire to stay with the same job for years, but the variety within the job, the customers you have contact with, or the travel opportunities may well satisfy your hare needs.

Hares require change and stimulation. Turtles require security and consistency. Hares are extroverts and creative. Turtles are introverts and methodical. If you are using your inventive mind, that's hare energy. When you become cautious and methodical, you tap into your turtle. Outwardly you may appear to be a hare when in truth, you feel like a turtle. A woman might perceive her partner as a turtle while his associates at work experience him as a hare. Similarly others may identify you as all turtle from the professional role in which they have come to know you, but you may feel and act like a hare in every other area.

I always gave the impression that I welcomed a challenge, sought after change and adjusted to it easily. As a writer I appeared to take creative risks despite the rejections, chase new ideas, and immerse myself in projects, some of which never got off the ground. I often behaved and sounded altogether like a hare. In truth however, few knew that in the aspect of home and motherhood, I was a devoted turtle. Our lifestyle shift to Muskoka sent me into worry over my childrens' social adjustment, our finances, and my ability to balance career aspirations with my need to be there for my family.

Regardless of how the world sees you, what primary personality type do you feel you really are? As you read the list of turtle and hare qualities, let your intuition tell you which ones best describe you. Ask yourself if you think you are primarily one or the other, a turtle or a hare. You may be both.

Turtles

Positive qualities expressed by Turtle:

- Organized and good at keeping to routine.
- Less apt to rush in work, speech and other areas.
- Good problem solver.
- Calm in crisis. Level-headed.
- Good with money. Often thrifty or a saver.
- Responsible. Able to bear a heavy load.
- Committed, loyal and steadfast to work and family.
- Stable. Needs and craves security.
- Task oriented. Stick-to-it type.
- Often conventional or traditional.
- Detail-oriented. Has a methodical mind.
- Meets due dates easily.
- Punctual. Always on time.
- Rational and logical. Left-brain thinker.
- Thinks before acting.
- Has sustained energy. Can work for long periods of time.
- Extremely hard worker. Willing to put in long hours.
- In control.
- Determined and often assertive.
- Slow to anger. Thinks before reacting.

Negative qualities expressed by Turtle:

- Not adventuresome.
- Sometimes too schedule-oriented or rigid with time.
- Can be stubborn.
- Awkward when out of comfort zone.
- May appear to be too serious or to worry too much.
- Can be plodding.
- May give impression of being boring.
- Usually hides feelings. Sometimes too restrained.
- May be too negative or too cautions.

- Demanding on self and others.
- Can be short-sighted.
- Reluctant to confront issues (hides in his shell).
- May be too controlling of self and others.

Hares

Positive qualities expressed by Hare:

- A good communicator.
- Willing to take risks.
- Idea and vision-oriented.
- Adventuresome. Loves excitement, travel, the unknown.
- Sociable. Mixes easily with many types of people.
- Goal or outcome-oriented.
- Unconventional.
- Extroverted.
- Entrepreneurial.
- Fun-loving and spontaneous.
- Has an inventive mind. Creative and intuitive.
- Passionate and enthusiastic.
- Multi-talented.
- Open and responsive.
- Quick-witted and humorous.
- Works hard at things he or she likes.
- Sometimes an idealist or dreamer.
- Often a right-brain thinker.
- Very generous in spirit.
- Many hobbies and interests.

Negative qualities expressed by Hare:

- May not think things through. Impulsive.
- Reacts too quickly. Compulsive.
- May be quick to anger or impatient.
- Sometimes restless, dissatisifed, indecisive.
- Sometimes nervous or agitated.
- Sometimes pretentious or grandiose.
- May spend money too easily.
- May scatter energy or be unfocused. Easily distracted.
- Bold and confident outwardly, fearful underneath.
- Often unrealistic.

- Gets too busy with too many things.
- May be disorganized and messy. Dislikes detail.
- Susceptible to burn-out from not pacing tasks.

Are You Both Turtle and Hare?

Inside each primary turtle there lives a hare.
Inside each primary hare there lives a turtle.

Just as introverts often hide their inner extrovert and vice versa, so is it also with turtles and hares. In a true hare there lives a turtle, in the true turtle there also lives a hare. Sometimes we are unaware of these counterparts in ourselves, and have not taken time to develop them. But often these strong counterpersonalities just need our conscious permission to come out.

Whether we are aware of it or not, most turtle types must have their hare come out at times, most hare types need their turtle at times. Turtle energy helps a hare work long hours, face sorting through the garage or figure out the year end's tax return. Our counterpart can surprise us suddenly. We may believe ourselves to be a dyed-in-the-wool turtle until we approach our fortieth birthday, then suddenly take a giant risk and try sky-diving.

Others know that it is their hare who loves to be stimulated with food and drink. "My hare has no self-control on the weekend, and I continually overindulge," my friend Ann complained. Another friend is a hare through and through, until the topic of child-rearing is discussed. Immediately her views shift to that of a very conservative turtle.

True turtles are also not without their surprises. Whereas generally they try to avoid risk in most areas, many turtles live in conservative business attire from nine-to-five, yet have their pilot's license or interest themselves in thoroughbred racing.

In small but significant ways, your counterpersonality comes to the fore. It's a little like walking with a shadow or twin, your other personality is with you at all times.

Turtles Are Reluctant to Say They Dream

Turtles rarely refer to themselves as dreamers. And some turtles don't believe they have dreams at all.

"I'm not a dreamer, nope. I dream at night, mind you, but I can definitely say that I don't think about the kind of dreams you're talking about," my friend Dick told me.

"C'mon, Dick," I answered. "Of course, you dream."

"Nope, Angie," he insisted. "I don't have dreams."

"You dream about catching that Muskie you've been after for years, don't you?" I asked.

"Sure, I do, and I plan to try again this year."

"And don't you read everything you can about Muskies, and think about what you'll need in supplies for the trip, then buy the new fishing line for it and talk about it with your buddies every time you get together over cards? I'd say that was a dream of yours you'd like to see fulfilled. Isn't that right?"

"I guess when you put it that way, you could call wanting to catch a Muskie, a dream. I've chased it long enough, and I'm not about to quit!"

Dick finally admitted to me that he, too, had a dream.

Because my friend honestly believes that he will succeed one day, we can't call his annual trip with his high hopes a fantasy. And since he has already put so much planning, patience and creative energy into the effort, we can't really call it a wish either. Until he catches a huge northern lake Muskie, it remains his personal dream.

Because Dick is a turtle, however, he still refers to this in "planners language" when he tells me, "I aim to get that Muskie this year!"

Hares Think in Possibilities,
Turtles Think in Practicalities

Turtles often restrain their dreaming through their use of cautious language. From turtles one hears terms such as projects, plans, strategies and goals. When turtles invest, one hears them talk about investment portfolios. When they retire, it is a retirement plan.

Hares free up their dreams through expansive and inflated language. From hares one hears terms such as mission statement, visions, creative concepts and entrepreneurial spirit. When hares retire, they make reference to their dream home or island in the sun.

Sometimes turtles and hares are actually saying the same thing but in different turtle and hare languages.

How We Feel About Our Turtle and Hare

My friend Shirley says, "My hare has to slow down and ride on my turtle's back these days. And even though we get things done, it feels too slow. My hare gets so impatient." Shirley admits to frequently being angry with her turtle because it hasn't allowed her to be spontaneous enough. She thinks of her hare as the enthusiastic child within; the one who frequently gets cheated of the fun. Conditioned from childhood to give up this happier part of herself, Shirley feels that her practical and plodding adult turtle has put a damper on the magic of her child hare.

Frustrated by turtle energy, my friend wants her hare back. She also recognizes, however, that she needs her turtle in order to finish writing the novel that's been waiting in her bureau for some free time. These days as she continues to write, Shirley tells me that turtle now carries hare on her back, and that she is making peace with the old anger she has always felt for turtle, and is finally utilizing her turtle strengths in ways that are not negative.

Another friend feels that hares are "artsy-fartsy" and turtles are "real." Bill enjoys being around hares but relates far better to fellow turtles.

I also used to become frustrated with turtles, especially my turtle. A turtle wasn't fast enough or exciting enough for me. And I was impatient with Turtle's slow speech. Often I was tempted to finish sentences for Turtle before he had had the chance to fully express his thoughts. As far as I was concerned, turtles worried too much about details and accuracy and too little about ideas and creativity. When I began to notice this turtle trait emerge in my writing, my hare went wild with impatience.

Most of all, turtles irritated me for being so downright content to putter along and do their tasks at the steady little pace that turtles like. For example, I often observed David happily sorting through his enormous tackle box, unraveling lines, poking through weights and lures, taking inventory. That this activity could be considered relaxing took me a long time to understand. These days I compare it to the same enjoyment I get from sorting through, placing and rearranging my photo albums.

Reflecting back, I now recognize that my younger hare was arrogant. I did utilize turtle energy, but begrudgingly, and only when absolutely necessary. Most of the time I got by on hare spurts. It was Hare who made it through university, was able to zoom through the house for a quick clean, and was a great crash dieter. And Hare was especially good at writing to deadline until the early hours of the morning. I used to like my inner hare.

Paradoxically, I also disliked my inner hare, more than turtle. My much younger hare used to quit a well-paying job because she was bored, be too frank and open, and sometimes too trusting. I found that Hare often took bold leaps and then would have difficulty later finding safe ground. And for years my hare was extremely vain.

Turtle was never such a problem, for I simply ignored whatever he urged me to do. That included, of course, whatever my turtle friends and family advised me as well.

Reconciling my inner turtle and hare, in whatever context I understood them, was my challenge. So also was it a challenge to reconcile Turtle and Hare when we they were mirrored outside of me, in the people I met, loved, lived and worked with.

When Hares Are Unfocused and Turtles Plod

Hare, becoming very excited, shoots off at the start of any race or goal, only to tire himself out quickly because he's put all his energy out, all at once.

She decides to write a book, then runs to her friends to discuss it, runs to the library for a little research, runs to the store to buy computer paper, runs back home to clean and organize her writing space in order to be able to write. Then Hare sees this patch of moss under a big shady tree and thinks, "Wouldn't it be so lovely, I must lie down, so tired of running around, I can't be like those turtles who keep plodding with those boring details, must save my energy for the big things."

But the book doesn't get written, and soon it's six months later, and time has ticked by in tasks that Hare can't even recall. That's also about the time Hare notices how much Turtle has accomplished in the meantime. The deck that Turtle has built around the pool, the garden that is already planted. All are concrete indications, visible signs of the progress and order everywhere in Turtle's life.

Hare is inwardly envious of Turtle, but doesn't have any inkling of how to become a little more like him. "Just to start," she thinks to herself.

Maybe she can manage it in the beginning, like the diet she began last year, the fitness membership she committed to this year and rarely uses. Ultimately it all strikes Hare as so very difficult and so boring. She really doesn't understand how Turtle can live his life the way he does. Frankly, sometimes she doesn't even like Turtle.

If you are a primary turtle, slow and sure as you are, as and wonderful as the route to the village is, perhaps you are reluctant to deviate from the course you have carved out for yourself unless you have a good hare around.

And if you are a primary hare, as wonderful as that little rest was in the shady part of the tree, it is sometimes easier to harness your impulsive side when you have a good turtle around to keep you on track.

What the hare gains in spurts and starts along the way is sometimes sacrificed in stability and sure-footedness. What the turtle gains in staying with goals on his agenda, he may sacrifice in his inability to enjoy life or have a good belly laugh. Take a turtle and put him on his back, and you don't see him laughing. When turtles are forced to lie on their backs, both literally and figuratively, they are in distress. This includes both ill bedridden turtles, as well as workaholic turtles, trying to relax on vacation.

When Turtles and Hares Become Fearful

In animal symbology, hares are known to represent nervous energy and fear. Expressions such as "running scared as a rabbit" come to mind. When a hare is frightened, it runs. When hares are angered they can be most verbal about it. Being natural communicators, it is very "hare" to be able to express their criticism most articulately. Angry turtles are often blunt and to the point. Anger, however, is sometimes a cover for unexpressed fear. When dreamers and planners feel tense and angry much of the time, it may be that fear is not being acknowledged.

In business, Hares are fearful they will lose ground and it will all be taken away from them. Often they are just too busy trying to keep up with the one too many things they have taken on. And hare types who become caught up in fear become impulsive and erratic, making foolish decisions without appropriate forethought.

Hare people are generally extroverts, thus more transparent by nature. This makes fear all that more apparent in hares. A reaction is almost immediate when a hare instantly flees, with a look of wide-eyed fear. One of my giveaway hare responses is the habit of speaking too quickly when I am nervous. Another destructive impulse I struggle with, when I am inwardly agitated, is an immediate hare leap towards the pantry for something sweet.

Only when hares learn to remain grounded and to develop a sense of inner control with help from their turtle, can behaviour change. The immediate impulse, however, is often "escape."

Turtles, by their very ability to hide under their shell for protection are able to conceal their fear more effectively. Expressions such as "withdraw into her shell" are common.

When turtles are fearful, their first reaction is to plant their legs a little more firmly into the ground and keep plodding even harder, secretly hoping things will straighten out in time. Turtles just simply aren't able to run away as fast as hares and, when push comes to shove, they pull back into their protective shells. This makes them appear even more introverted or shy.

I have a turtle friend who, when under pressure or fearful, develops an intense stare as if deep in thought. Her shoulders become quite physically pulled together and hunched as she goes about her business.

Money is often an important issue of fear for turtles and hares. Turtles are often attracted to hares for their generous gift-giving nature, and hares appreciate the fact that turtles generally clear their debts. When money becomes scarce, however, both turtles and hares can be equally pre-occupied with money, worrying how the other either holds on to it more tightly or spends it. The very quality which at first attracts one to the other, later becomes an irritation between them. Turtles then may brood about what they perceive as the irresponsible spending habits of hares and hare may come to resent the way turtles hold tight to their pursestrings. Fear around scarcity and money can create destructive over-reactions in turtles and hares.

Hares and Turtles in Relationships

Despite their differences, hares attract turtles and turtles are fascinating to hares. Confused and bemused by their mates' habits and ways, turtles and hares spend a lifetime and untold energy trying to change and understand one another. This holds true whether they cohabit, are friends, business partners or they marry. And judging from divorce statistics, turtles married to hares, more often than not lose the battle to harmonize their diverse natures, only to remarry and repeat the pattern with yet a different turtle or hare.

Aside from the obvious cliche about opposites attracting, I wondered why turtles and hares were so powerfully drawn to one another?

I concluded that many of the inner turtle or hare qualities which I had difficulty expressing or needed, I brought into my life through my relationships. For example, in college I had a conscientious turtle girlfriend with whom I worked in the library, and another who motivated me to attend weekly yoga. Otherwise I might have procrastinated. And whatever I was in awe of, I also noticed; the tremendous discipline that my partner David applied to his life; the clean kitchen of one turtle friend; the way another hare friend spontaneously played on the floor with his children. Friends and family remained a mirror of my potential, as I hoped in time to acquire these qualities in myself.

Similarly, whatever hare or turtle quality I disliked or judged badly in myself, I also saw mirrored. The truth was that the behaviours which bothered me most, were the things I was prone to do myself. This accounted for why I nagged my children for being messy, and why I tried to convince my mate to quit smoking.

Money Issues in Turtle and Hare Relationships

If money is an issue for one partner it is only a question of time before it becomes an issue for the relationship.

If money is *not* an issue for one partner, but a decided issue with the other, it will only be a question of time before money intrudes. This is true for any two people who are in a working relationship, whether it be in love, friendship, or business. It is in the daily commonplace incidences that our most fundamental attitudes come to the fore; our willingness to be the first to put coins in the parking meter; when we offer to buy an ice cream cone for the child of a friend; when we save both the small as well as larger receipts for tax purposes.

The individual for whom money holds the strongest power or significance, will inevitably bring his "relationship" to money to his present partnership or friendship. When this happens, turtles and hares may become watchful about signs of generosity, pettiness, or secrecy. Eventually, one's own natural response to money may become exaggerated or repressed, creating reactions that are simply over-reactions until everyone appears to act "out of character." For example, when money becomes an issue between a generous hare and a withholding turtle, Hare may eventually withhold as well.

Equally destructive is a situation in which one partner begins to feel that love and money are equated; that is to say that the degree of caring is proportionate to the degree of generosity. If this is so, core beliefs around self-worth, material attachments and money as an expression of caring need to be reevaluated and resolved.

The Dangers of Turtle and Hare Laziness

We like to let our partner take care of what we have been reluctant to develop or have chosen not to learn.

We may live with our counterpart because unconsciously we may want to live out those parts of ourselves that we have not yet sufficiently developed. To help ourselves feel complete, and because we simply need this in our life, we bring these qualities into our lives through our partners and friends. We may even hope to learn from them. Thus, a shy turtle, who secretly wishes to become more gregarious, marries a hare. And a disorganized hare relies on a turtle mate to have things in hand on moving day.

The danger, however, is settling into a turtle/hare laziness in the relationship. Whereas you began by really valuing turtle and hare qualities in your partner, you now completely rely on them. In time, this may come to mean that you no longer do this for yourself, even though before the relationship, you were perfectly capable of tapping into aspects of your inner hare or turtle and accomplishing these things.

Mary used to procrastinate on arranging car repairs, mowing the lawn and weeding the garden. She also had a distaste for reviewing insurance bills, income tax receipts and folding laundry. Over time, as her husband willingly took on these tasks, she became less appreciative of his efforts, almost apathetic.

This may be one of the biggest areas of resentment in turtle/hare relationships. Unless both individuals in the partnership agree and understand what is expected of themselves and the other, resentment will build up. For example, if your turtle and hare roles are not balanced, and you are consistently placed in a turtle role, you may begrudge the fact that your turtle is always burdened with the finances, or that your partner is continually leaving the organizing to you. If you are a hare, you will resent it if your turtle partner has become a social recluse or you have to do all the communicating in the relationship.

We Seek Support from Our Counterparts

What we unconsciously fear or worry about may be voiced
by our partners or friends.

We look for support from our friends and partners, particularly when they can bring a fresh perspective to an issue. What we most often need to hear is an affirmation that our primary turtle or hare is on track. Sometimes, however, instead of encouragements we receive instead counterviews that feel more like sabotage than support.

When we receive opposing thoughts it may be difficult to remember that our partner's or friend's primary energy is opposite to ours. And even though they may have the best of intentions, it may not always be communicated just in the way we need to hear it. What we may be *hearing* are simply the echoes of our own inner turtle and hare doubts, especially when we have conflicting thoughts over an issue. What we unconsciously fear or worry about may be voiced by those with whom we share our thoughts.

Ellen saw this each time she approached Neil with a new "hare-brained" inspired idea. Completely off the wall in her enthusiasm, she came out with her ideas so that Neil too could share in the vision. Secretly she wanted the approval of a turtle, to tell her that this was no fly-by-night wish or fantasy. She also needed his energy to generate more excitement for the project.

Fully plugged into his logical and practical turtle mode, Neil presented no-nonsense counter-viewpoints which seemed to oppose several of Ellen's ideas. In turn, Ellen felt that this created immediate roadblocks to her original vision, even though he may have been correct in his logic. Neil maintained that he was simply trying to protect her, but to Ellen, it felt like sabotage anyway. His down-to-earth approach became a damper for Ellen's hare, and what began as a wonderful discussion sometimes ended in an argument in which two people were defending their turtle and hare ideas.

We work with, play with, and love an assortment of hare and turtle friends and partners; some are primary dreamers, some are planners. But how wonderful if Hare and Turtle could truly take the journey together, arriving at the village gate, not with a hollow sense of having missed some important thing along the way, but in the spirit of having shared the journey, as companions, assisting and supporting one another along the way.

Living Out of Character

We all have a basic true nature with which we feel most comfortable. If we choose, we can make life more interesting by switching roles now and again in order to develop our inner turtle or hare. But what about those individuals who are living their lives, totally "out of character?"

Trying to live a hare's life when you are essentially a turtle guarantees you tension and unhappiness. Similarly, to harness a hare and expect him to think and behave like a turtle, feels oppressive and is pure misery for any hare. There may be more turtles and hares stuck in being unable to express their true natures than we realize. This I believe is true of turtles and hares within marriages, friendships, families and in business. Turtles and hares often allow themselves to be influenced in destructive ways.

My friend Jenny, a city hare, allowed her partner to talk her into life on a farm. Jenny's quiet inner turtle responded and fell in love with the beauty and quiet of the rolling hills and the large white farmhouse with the green shutters. Jenny, however, felt isolated during winters, and didn't much like the constant responsibility of the large vegetable garden and the farm animals.

Because they were close to a festival town, Jenny's husband also had the notion to register the farm as a Bed and Breakfast. What began as a country retreat ended up representing long hours of labour for Jenny, whose personality was rapidly, and unwillingly, becoming entirely turtle. When Jenny eventually began to express her needs, her partner became controlling, resisting any changes Jenny wished to make to restimulate her inner hare. Once she became committed to do so, the marriage ended.

Although it became clearly necessary for Jenny to leave her marriage, those relationships which can more easily adjust to shifts in roles thrive and often deepen, despite turtle and hare role reversals.

Another dramatic role shift which can happen is when hares reluctantly, or even voluntarily, put their career on the back burner to become stay-at-home mothers. For the right turtle or hare, working at home may be the ideal niche she is looking for. For the fifteen years in which I worked from my home, on the whole, it felt right for me. Our house became a base from which my hare could spin into many inner and outer directions: classes in clay; my writing pursuits; a home consulting business. It would be unrealistic to maintain that there were no periods in which my hare felt buried by the many turtle responsibilities that the earlier years of mother-hood demanded, but that too seemed to shift whenever I immersed myself in a new direction.

For others, who may have left careers and professions built up over time, and in which there had been much satisfaction, the 180 degree turn to a full-time domestic lifestyle with its daily dirt cycle, may simply be too much. The adjustment is not for everyone to make, and need not be irrevocable.

When One Partner Chooses to Switch Roles

When turtles and hares live together, because each knows intuitively what the other's primary energy is, the relationship may fall into a pattern where the couple, despite little battles to change one another, also knows what each can expect. Time passes, and their respective roles are more or less accepted. But life events and a career move may bring about a change. One partner may choose to alter his role: if he was formerly a turtle, he now becomes a hare or vice versa. This may bring about a marital crisis as both partners try to re-establish equilibrium to the relationship. After all, one member of the partnership has brought in a whole new "animal."

Although the pendulum has swung, throwing the couple temporarily out of their comfort zone, it may in fact be a necessary shift. But some relationships cannot bear the change.

"Is it harder for a hare to change and become a turtle or for a turtle to become a hare?" I asked my friend Alice, a tried-and-true turtle at heart.

"Even if I wanted to change overnight, it's the external influences, especially my family, that would make it most difficult to become a hare now," Alice answered. "There's a lot of societal and family approval to be gained from being a turtle. My family has become accustomed to me being a turtle: predictable, stable, organized. I'm aware of my patterns, but continue even now to give them what they want, in an effort to live up to their expectations."

Alice had a good point, but as a hare, I needed to emphasize to her as well, how hard it had been for me to change into a turtle, too. I explained that I had tried to be a turtle on and off all my life, and had just not been able manage it. "Developing and staying with discipline in any area of my life has been the difficulty for me," I confided. "In order to get out of doing what I know I need to be doing, I can come up with the most noble distractions."

Alice maintained that when a hare wants to become a turtle, the family is relieved. "Not so the other way. When I, the all-time classic turtle, get the notion to let my hare out, all hell breaks out," she said.

"It's easier for them to have you keep thinking and behaving as a turtle than to accept you primarily as a hare, because then they don't have to do the mundane chores when you do your hare-thing. The underlying message is *stay just the way you are*. No turtle or hare is immune to that pressure," Alice emphasized.

What the family doesn't understand perhaps is that when true turtles allow themselves to become hares, there is less to fear than one might think. When turtles allow their inner hare out, they generally do not lose their conscientious and responsible nature. Rather, they often become a more relaxed and spontaneous turtle family member, and that can be very freeing for everyone.

Ultimately, it becomes a goal for turtles and hares to know the positive and negative qualities of their true natures, whether it be turtle energy or hare energy. They must also be willing and able to adapt and utilize the counter quality when it is required. If we can draw on the qualities of both our inner hare or inner turtle, then we do not need to have someone else do that for us. Thus we now have ample inner resources to be both a dreamer and a planner.

Turtles and Hares in Business

Hares have a hard time believing their limits; Turtles have a hard time believing they are smart.

My friend Valerie is an executive turtle and considers herself a "professional doer."

"My director, an executive hare, bounces his ideas off me. I'm the critical assessor, who brings the practical ramifications to the discussion. What he likes is to know it will be done, and done right."

Valerie explained, "To be an executive turtle breeds confidence because the results of the doing are very visible. When turtles and hares start off in business, hares have a hard time believing their limits, turtles have a hard time believing they are smart."

Turtles are sometimes so task-oriented they leave little time to smell the flowers for themselves. Secretly, they may wish they had the get-up-and-go of the hare, whose spurts of energy give him the time to take his opportunities underneath the tree.

"Maybe some of this hare energy can be learned," Turtle wonders as he crosses the finish line, a winner, yes, but thirsty and bone weary. Despite the fact that his best effort has brought him big rewards, he has begun to recognize aspects of joylessness in his life. Such committed turtles often rise to great positions; many putting in long and arduous hours as they climb to positions of power and respect in business.

Hares can accomplish great things in a variety of fields. They speculate well and have created dynamic careers in private business, as well as shining in such areas as sales and marketing. Hares are known for their diverse talents and they work hard and efficiently when they love their work.

The more your work demands of your hare, the less you need to live Hare out in your private life; the more Turtle your work is, the more your hare needs stimulation.

Some businesses, by their sheer nature or function, demand almost 100% turtle or 100% hare from us. Tasks which require assembly or a repetitive routine leave little stimulation for a hare in a turtle job. In such cases, hare activities must be sought after hours.

Years ago, Jonathan functioned as more than 75% turtle in the family business. He compensated by travelling a lot and participating in winter and summer sports activities. Later, after a career shift that involved more speculation, longer hours, employee and product frustrations, Jonathan had become 75% hare at work, and desired little else than to relax on the couch after dinner.

Regardless of whether the nature of the business is essentially turtle or hare, the launching of any first-time business or new risk, requires the resiliency and enterprising energy of the hare. At the same time, it needs turtle commitment and vigilance to survive its early growing pains. That means that a turtle in business must learn entrepreneurial qualities to get going, yet hold onto enough turtle qualities to establish her security. A hare must also develop turtle discipline. Ideally, Hare needs to hire strong turtle employees to assist in the building of the business. Later, when established, both a hare and turtle can allow the pendulum to swing back to middle-ground so that their true natures may be expressed better.

Turtles and hares reach their "level of incompetence"
when they must work in positions that are
out of character to their natures.

If you see yourself turning into a "couch-potato" on weekends or are beginning to use substances such as food, alcohol and cigarettes to cope, you may need to re-evaluate how you are living out your turtle and hare.

PART 3

The Wheel of Wisdom

Who Is Owl?

Fairy stories often have an animal or small character who is both detached yet involved, and is seen as the "bridge" between the main characters of the story; a symbol of one who oversees the situation and has a real understanding of what is going on. In "The Turtle and the Hare," Owl is such a bridge and symbol, a metaphor for wisdom. Owl embodies the best qualities of both Turtle and Hare.

Each of us was born with owl wisdom, but regrettably have unlearned it. We have become turtles and hares instead. Owl wisdom is intuitive and practical, creative and grounded. It is both methodical and imaginary, realistic and visionary, meditative and spontaneous. With discipline, patience, experience and knowledge, all of us can rediscover our innate owl wisdom. When we tap into owl wisdom, we become wise turtles and wise hares.

WISDOM 1

The Differences Between Wishes, Dreams and Fantasies

The greatest achievement was at first and for a time a dream.
The oak sleeps in the acorn; the bird waits in the egg;
and in the highest vision of the soul a waking angel stirs.
Dreams are the seedlings of realities.
JAMES ALLEN

Wishes Are the Seeds of Dreams

Like wildflowers, wishes emerge all by themselves. They propagate effortlessly. Pay attention to a child like Sara and you begin to understand the abundant nature of wishes. And if, like dandelions that have gone to seed, we can blow a balloon of wish seeds into the universe, some will scatter aimlessly and die but a few will land on a fertile piece of ground and germinate.

This propagation strategy, which is to produce many, many seeds in order to ensure the germination of some, is an interesting metaphor when applied to wishes. Children are spontaneous with wishes. Adults, who have not lost this ability, will still wish on a star, throw pennies in a fountain and believe in wish walls. They know, however, that not all wishes will be realized but, like the blown seeds of dandelions, wishes are sent out as whispers to drift wherever they may find themselves.

Wishes Attract Themselves to Other Wishes

"Be careful what you wish for, it might just come true" is a saying I've paid attention to. Be mindful to express your wishes with some forethought. My experience has been that wishes have their own power and, as single thoughts, they gather energy. Perhaps like small energy fields, wishes attract themselves to other wishes.

When wishes have conscious intention behind them, they become strong wish seeds. And when these wishes germinate, they become the seedlings of dreams.

A Good Fantasy Is a Wish With a Storyline

Fantasy, and the ability to fantasize, is often a positive asset. Some people believe that the purpose of fantasy is to keep it in the realm of the unattainable.

"Fantasies are supposed to be imaginary daydreams of things that could never be," my friend Doug maintains. "I fantasize about driving a Porsche but know I'm not likely ever to have one. It gives me a lot of pleasure to dream about it though."

Seeing fantasies as fictitious daydreams that have little connection to reality but as an enjoyable pastime is one viewpoint. Fantasies can enliven our otherwise too comfortable or boring day-to-day lives. The approach I like, however, is to think of fantasy as the integral part of my creative imagination.

Creative fantasy is active imagination playing with itself. Through the use of active daydreaming, we can let ideas spin out fantasies that not only entertain us, but can be useful in visualizing where a dream might wish to take us. Our imagination can take us through a "dry run" of the dream, allowing us to visualize it step by step in order to check it out first with our thoughts and feelings.

If the fantasy "feels good," then we may be on the right track to a potentially fulfilling dream. If the fantasy "feels real," then we are close to a dream that has potential for actualization and is not too far fetched.

Now take the storyline, chisel away the details that were fun to imagine but seem too unlikely to materialize, and you have a part-dream or a portion of the fantasy you can make into your dream. What simply remains to be worked out is a plan to a sound, reachable goal.

My fantasy for years has been to own a beach house. My imagination knows what the sand will be like, and that I will go for early morning walks to beachcomb. I also think about whether this house will be on the west or east coast, and take armchair trips with my atlas to daydream over coves and coastlines. I visualize my sundeck where I will drink tea and write in my journal. And so I have opened a beach house bank account, and have fun with the customer service prepresentatives at my bank, whenever I make a small deposit in it.

In truth, this fantasy is part of my larger dream, which includes writing, teaching, family, water and freedom. I've chiseled out the fanciful details and, although I have modified the dream considerably, for now I still plan to live near water. I have meshed the fantasy with the dream. And it feels right.

Don't Confuse Wishes and Fantasies With the Dream

Don't let the fulfillment of one wish or fantasy sidetrack you from your dream. When wishes or fantasies are fulfilled along the way, you may be deluded into a kind of "dream lethargy," in which you lose the motivation to complete your dream journey. Don't confuse your wishes and fantasies with the larger plan and dream. Don't let the achievement of smaller wishes distract you from your larger goal. Enjoy them. Relax and take pleasure in them, but clearly see them as rewards that have been given *en route* to the dream.

I Want It, But God, Please Don't Give It to Me

Some people prefer to keep the fantasy as fantasy, rather than achieve the dream. Making a fantasy "real" is far less fun for some individuals than the pleasurable experience of the pure daydream. Bringing a dream to fruition takes discipline and hard work after all.

Others think of the fantasy as a goal which, once reached, only leaves the lingering question, *Now what?* "I want it but, God, please don't give it to me!" is the unspoken prayer.

A dream in a fantasy state saves us from confronting fears, issues and vague uncertainties. Fantasies keep the dreamer engaged without boredom. We can think in terms of *What if?* and let our imagination carry us away to scenes in which we play a leading role. To lose the fantasy would mean we would to have to replace it, an unthinkable prospect if the fantasy has an emotional hold on us. This is especially so if we deeply desire the fantasy and yet fear it might come true if steps were taken towards it.

The conflict between the fantasy of being a published writer and the fear of rejection has kept many a manuscript in a dusty drawer for years. Dreaming of entering a competition and missing the application deadline may be disappointing, but it still leaves room for the fantasy of "next time." Or we may hear friends talk and plan the perfect retirement, only to witness later their disillusionment with the life style. Stories such as these feed our doubts that the dream will not ultimately satisfy us. We may unconsciously dread achieving our dream. The worry looms: What if we make the fantasy our dream, and get it, and the dream doesn't live up to our expectations?

This is a fear that may need to be confronted. If the fantasy has a powerful longing attached to it and speaks to a soul need, is it not better to take it out into *real life,* and experience it with no regrets?

A Good Dream Is Expansive

Fantasies thought about repetitively, that are narrowly focused but have a needy or urgent quality to them, may become obsessions. Obsessed about long enough, we may act on these thoughts and turn fantasy into compulsion. Fantasies about model-thin beauty create compulsive eating disorders for weight control. Fantasies about acquiring material comforts create compulsive workaholism. Such behaviour may have an addictive edge to it, moving life into a smaller sphere within an isolated, unreal and destructive world.

Good fantasies enhance your life and are expansive. They are a part of a dream continuum that spirals out and upwards. You begin with a wish, give it energy, then create a fantasy. You set in motion step-by-step goals, spinning wishes, plans, dreams and fantasies into one spiral vision. When the dream is fulfilled, you can come back to its source, feeling complete and ready to nurture the seed of a new wish. Great dreams and plans need the energy of good wishes and fantasies.

Don't Let Your Dream Get Ahead of Your Plan

In the fable, Hare bounded off ahead and left Turtle in the dust. Don't let your active imagination, your fear, or your vision run away on its own and leave your hard-working turtle and plan back there somewhere, plodding at the starting point trying to catch up.

I have known dreamers (and I am one) who, before they were able to take their dream and align it with a manageable plan, got carried away and allowed their imagination to spin off fantastic visions. That is not to imply that even grandiose visions do not have a place in the dream. But you must not instantly overwhelm your practical turtle if you are planning a grand journey, or he simply won't join you. Leave that long-range goal a little further along the path.

To understand a run-away hare, picture your hare imagination leading you and the dream like the *Roadrunner* cartoon bird. This funny, energetic bird speeds way ahead, so fast that he runs off the cliff and drops. This crash to "earth awareness" can be disheartening to a dreamer. And if the plan was your trail, and you have lost it, you may need to retrace your steps to get back to it in, order to carry on with the dream.

To illustrate, visualize this scenario. You make a marvelous honey mustard that friends rave about and beg for a sample at Christmas. Finally they have convinced you that you must market it. Full of new plans, you rush to visit your best friend to share the news. You will renovate your kitchen to inspection standards and supply the mustard to the farmers' markets in the area. It will, of course, have its own unique label and name. Delicatessens will also sell your product and, within the year, your line will expand to include your superb summer mustard pickles. Then you will need to find an investor so that you can have a factory, a means to distribute nationally, and a sales specialist, who will open the door to sell to a major grocery chain store.

You have spun a dream out for yourself in fantastic detail. This is not altogether a bad thing to do. I am acquainted with a very successful businesswoman who swears by this method. She told me, "Sometimes, before I go to sleep, I lie in bed and try to visualize my dream in complete detail. I then imagine each step I must take to achieve it." She does her best "planning" before she goes to sleep. Then during the productive hours of her day, she begins the step-by-step "doing" of the specific stage she is at in the dream process. This woman has achieved some grand dreams in just this way.

But there you are, dreaming about gourmet mustard and having difficulty coming back down to the first step in the context of your life as it is today. Beginning by renovating your kitchen seems like a messy (and expensive) chore. You will need to keep your job until production and sales get off the ground. Prosperity will take a lot of mustard. You don't confide these doubts to the friend you have shared this with but, by the end of the visit, you are already feeling discouraged.

Don't allow your hare to take your turtle too far too quickly. If you are a large and expansive dreamer, it becomes even more essential to chart out a good dream map for yourself. At the start, Hare must slow down his pace to accommodate Turtle; then as you near the finish line, Turtle will have the endurance and power to motivate and help Hare finish the race.

What Kind of Dreamer and Planner Are You?

Do you have a dream? Do you have a plan? What is your goal? How likely are you to arrive at your destination? Is your goal realistic? Is it a hare whim? Or a turtle-organized investment plan? There are many types of dreamers and planners. What type are you?

Dreamer and Planner Types

The Make-Good Dreamer/Planner: Whether to herself or others, this dreamer often has something to "prove." Sometimes there is a feeling of "carrying the torch" for someone else; for example, an individual strives for academic credentials to please the parent who had this goal but did not fulfill it. The sense of responsibility is high and there may be a tendency to perfectionism or workaholism. Turtles often become *make-good dreamers*.

The Dream Junkie: This dreamer is the perpetual "Peter Pan" of dreamers, who may be so in love with dreaming that it leads to a sort of dream addiction. He may love the "high" of talking up the dream but lack the discipline to complete the dream and make it real. Full of himself and his ideas, and preferring a level of constant excitement, this dreamer never grows up and often lives life on an emotional dream roller coaster. Out-of-balance hares become *dream junkies*.

The Bite-Size Dreamer/Planner: This is a modest dreamer who is predisposed to caution (and perhaps a touch of pessimism), but wants to dream nevertheless. To buffer himself from possible failure or disappointment, this individual dreams "small" and in methodical and calculated stages. Only one goal at a time is focused on, rather than a grander long-term vision. Turtles make good *bite-size dreamers*.

The Entrepreneurial Dreamer/Planner: This is the risk-taking creative dreamer, who is often equally successful in business. Unlike the "bite-size dreamer," this individual is consistently attuned to the "big" picture and with discipline can bring great dreams to fruition. On the down side, *entrepreneurial dreamers* sometimes bite off more than they can chew. Inspired hares often make good *entrepreneurial dreamers*.

The War and Peace Dreamer/Planner: This dreamer has a "cause" orientation, is often involved in environmental or "green" issues, as well as being an activist for general social change. This individual may be found in missionary work as readily as lobbying at a political level. Both idealistic hares and practical turtles are attracted to causes and make committed *war and peace dreamers*.

The Don Quixote Dreamer: This "dream-the-impossible-dream" dreamer appears to be chasing windmills and living on fantasies. A pure idealist, this dreamer's motives reach beyond the ego, being sometimes spiritual or altruistic in nature. Appearing to have her head in the clouds, this individual may affiliate herself with the cause and remain a visionary with little support but for a few loyal "Sancho Panza" followers. Nevertheless, unlike the "junkie dreamer" who is bitten by many dreams, the *Don Quixote dreamer* may spend a lifetime following only one dream. Hares can make passionate *Don Quixote dreamers*.

The In-The-Closet Dreamer/Planner: This is the passive dreamer, who may secretly crave recognition or power but may fear or lack the motivation to act on his desires. An *in-the-closet dreamer* sometimes projects his ambitions or dreams onto his partner or children. This allows him to live out the dream with fewer direct personal risks. Many of these people become the driving force behind active dreamers, who would otherwise not be as successful alone. Some turtles are *in-the-closet dreamers,* as are timid hares.

The Lost Dreamer: This individual has forgotten how to dream and often believes that he does not desire a dream or is incapable of dreaming. Whether from early disillusion or conditioning, a *lost dreamer* has a "that's-the-way-it-is" approach, is sometimes stoic and resigned to his life, and has stopped growing. Sometimes this is a former dreamer who has long ago attained a dream but has not seeded new ones and has gone stale from lack of joy in life. Both turtles and hares can be *lost dreamers*.

WISDOM 2

What Is Your Dream?

I have learned this at least by my experiment:
That if one advances confidently in the direction of his dreams,
and endeavors to live the life which he has imagined,
he will meet with a success unexpected in common hours.
HENRY DAVID THOREAU

What Is Your Dream Really About?

We all have the ability to know what our fantasy is, but may not have taken the time to uncover the dream or be able to state it to ourselves in clear terms. A dream may not necessarily be about the Porsche that a friend or neighbour is driving, although that may be a part of the dream. More often, a dream is slow in being realized and less direct.

Some turtles don't believe that they dream at all. They may not know how to dream. But this will change as they come to understand that their planning often contains all the elements of a good dream. Turtles need to work at seeing the underlying dream in every plan, hares need to focus on the potential plan within every dream.

Every Dream Needs a Plan

It was some time ago, before the building of my office and the wish wall, that I heard myself complaining on the telephone to my friend Evelyn.

"I want to be a writer, but I just can't seem to make it happen for myself these days. I can't get excited or motivated enough to want to write about anything. I've got some good proposals in the drawer and they are important to me, but life is getting in the way. All I know is that I want to write and I have to come up with a plan soon."

"That's right," Evelyn answered in her cheerful drawl, *"every dream needs a plan."*

"That's a great idea, Evelyn, that's it! *every dream needs a plan*, that's what my new book will be about." Suddenly I was motivated. I had the dream, I needed a plan, and I was going to write about it.

Since that moment when Evelyn first coined the phrase, I have been trying to develop and live out my own dream plan.

When you are really ready to want the dream,
you will also be ready to plant the first seed of commitment,
that is, wanting and thinking about a plan.

A dream without a plan remains just that, a dream. The Roman playwright Seneca said, "Our plans miscarry because they have no aim. When a man does not know what harbour he is making for, no wind is the right wind."

Only when you begin to think in terms of a plan, do you begin to make progress. When you acquire the plan, you have also acquired your roadmap. And the journey has begun.

When Is a Dream For You?

When you see someone else living it. A good dream indicator might be when you know or see someone else doing something that triggers excitement or longing within you. If you find yourself continually observing an individual over a period of time or reading about them or perhaps you seek out people whose life-style you would wish for, take note. If you catch yourself thinking, "I could do that!" then you are getting close to a potential dream.

Years ago, I often made a point of going to author lectures. I would sit in the audience with the thought, "I would love to do that!" Not only was I interested in how writers worked and lived their lives, but afterwards, I would contemplate how they had communicated their ideas, what had motivated or inspired them and how might I have gone about achieving a similar goal. Desiring to live the writer's life didn't take hold of me overnight. The dream gradually found me as I continued to attend bookstore author signings, writers' conferences and library lecture series.

When you can visualize yourself living it. You know you have a good dream when you can daydream about it and see realistic details of your dream in your active imagination. I emphasize the word *realistic* because if you have built your dream on a lifestyle or profession, look again at the details of life under the surface.

Before I really understood what writers did, I was enchanted with the persona, reputation, aura, mystery, call it what you like, that surround most artists and writers.

One writer, when asked how he felt about his craft, simply said, "I love *having* written." For me, it was a revealing comment about his feelings regarding the nose-to-the-grindstone aspect of his chosen profession.

You need to be able to visualize yourself living out the juicy part of your dream while at the same time clearly acknowledging to yourself what it is about the dream that you do not like. Can you willingly commit to all of it?

This might be a good time to do a mental inventory. Create a minus and plus list as you think about your dream. Doing this now may save you grief or sabotage later.

When you have found a dream where the desire for the dream and the commitment you have made to it is more important than the outcome. It has been said that success is a journey, not a destination. If you share this belief, then your effort alone is what counts. In other words, is the fulfillment or outcome of the dream the lone requirement to your happiness or does the idea of the dream and the prospect of going for this goal create enormous pleasure for you also?

For example, as a writer, I enjoy attending and giving workshops. And when I'm not writing, I'm reading and researching. If not that, I'm thinking about writing. I also enjoy talking about creative ideas, mine or yours, should you be interested. I'm always browsing in bookstores, reading book reviews, love watching writers being interviewed, love being interviewed. And more importantly, if I were not to be published again, I would still love language, storytelling, myths and symbols, and still continue to write and think of myself as a writer. Find yourself a dream where the journey is as satisfying as the goal.

When you want to give your dream top priority even if it's not always possible. Family, sex, laundry, spirituality, friendship, sun, water and one hundred other things continuously shift in priority and compete for attention. All must find their place in the dream as well. And rightly so. But you know you have a dream when it is consistently placed on the front burner as something you need to make time for. The reality of doing this may take timing and balance, but that's why it is so necessary to want the dream.

When this dream is yours and no one else's. It's easier to sustain wanting the dream if you truly own your own dream. It is not about someone else wanting or choosing the dream for you, or drawing you in to support their dream. If this is the case, resentment will likely build, towards the goal, yourself, and eventually also towards the individual who "dreamt you in" without the consent of your heart.

When the dream is truly yours, it is easy for your dream to have integrity because "your heart will be in it." The dream will have meaning for you, and you will be clear on what the attainment of the dream represents for you emotionally, spiritually and in a worldly sense.

When you understand what the dream is really about. I think and dream about the beach house I'm going to own on the coast, but is the dream really the beach house?

Most of our dreams center around several dominant themes. Perhaps these themes are really needs which recur until some longing is satiated. And can this longing be filled from something outside of ourselves or can it be met within?

Although an ocean retreat for someone else might represent simplicity, health or relaxation, it has come to symbolize the pinnacle of freedom for me. A freedom which I have not easily been able to give myself permission for in the past. This awareness has made the beach-house matter less, as I work on a plan which builds in more freedom in my day-to-day as well as a period of retreat time away, possibly near an ocean.

Give some thought to your dream and what needs this dream might satisfy. If your dream does have a hidden agenda, it is good to know it.

Primary themes in your life might be:

- Freedom
- Power/control
- Love
- Creativity
- Peace/contentment
- Security/safety
- Recognition/attention
- Spirituality

Wise turtles and hares know what the dream is really about.

When the dream has just enough vision to reach beyond you. A great dream is designed to satisfy the dreamer, but in some way it also goes beyond her to encompass some good for others. It represents no spiritual/material conflict, to the dreamer or to those the dream involves or impacts. Make the dream larger than yourself. You will find that in those moments when you become weary or lose faith in yourself, you immediately have another reason to return to the dream and fight for it.

Finally, there is no point in being able to envision the last step of the dream if you don't end up liking and respecting the main participant in the dream, *you*. A friend of mind told me, "I love the dream, but I don't like what I have to do for it."

Good dreams are about goodness, for you and others. They enhance life, not negate it. Good dreams make you and others feel a little bit taller.

Timing Is an Important Part of the Plan

You must ask yourself, "Is the timing advantageous for this dream right now?" There are a number of factors to consider here: circumstance, the economy, your personal financial status, children, geography and more.

A few years ago I had the opportunity to do food shows, and I loved the work. Management hired me as food stage master of ceremonies to other celebrity authors and chefs. At last I had the opportunity to work with other writers and to travel, but it felt very difficult to manage. I dreamt about doing more shows of this kind, and it appeared that I had opened a first door. I realized, however, that this dream meant periods of time away from home, and my children were very young. I had to make a choice and the conflict was clear. I now needed to rethink promises I had made to myself when I first had children and choose whether I wished to include a career in food and promotions. I opted to continue to write at home with minimal travel.

The offer passed me by and was lost. The timing had been all wrong. All I could wish for was that another, and perhaps equally good path, would show itself when I was ready.

But right timing has also smiled on me. The year I wrote and launched *Mad About Muffins*, women were also going mad for fitness books, lunch-hour workouts and healthy snacks. Muffins became a lunch-box favorite. Suddenly little muffin outlets were opening everywhere near office complexes and in shopping malls. These treats were giants and came in exciting varieties. As they caught on to replace the donut for many, so did my little cookbook. Good timing for my idea.

You need everything possible going for you in the plan, and right timing is a crucial key to success. To let your intuition guide you with timing takes more than a little belief in youself. Lack of confidence and inexperience is often at the root of poor dream planning early on. When in your heart you know that the timing is off, it takes courage not to develop an idea into a dream.

The fear may also be there that if you let this great idea pass by, there may not be another. When the door closes, that's it! This, too, requires a belief in your ability to attract new opportunities, and think of new concepts. Don't allow your hare to jump, only to regret the choice later.

An intuitive sense of good timing decreases the risk factor
in a new dream plan.
Poor timing increases risk.

I used to think that ideas were mysterious and magical. Well, admittedly, ideas are fun and special, but they are accessible to both turtles and hares. If your idea can't become a dream right now due to timing, then put the idea away, or better yet, give it away altogether. Someone is likely looking for it. Trust in your ability to draw on a wellspring of creativity inside of you.

I didn't always think this way. Years ago I worried that if I didn't act on a great idea, another one would never visit me again. How much better to believe, as one prolific writer expressed it, that all ideas regularly float by on a kind of imaginary "conveyor belt" in the sky. All great ideas and dreams are accessible to anyone who wishes to tap into this imaginary plane. As you see the idea, observe it and ask yourself if you want this one. If not, let it go for someone else to choose. Every now and then a dream will float by that will look very appealing to you. Perhaps this is the one you will take and manifest.

This process combines both a bit of dreaming and fantasizing, but if allowed, affirms that creative ideas are out there if you are willing to let them in and have the ability to manifest them.

Allow yourself to speculate for a moment on this notion. What if ideas, like you, have their own energy field, and hover around those people who might bring the idea into form? In other words, if you have the impulse to bring creativity into form, then perhaps creative ideas also look to be manifested. If that concept is not too far-fetched for you, then is it possible that just as we "create" or choose an idea, it, too, may be looking to also choose its "creator"? And when that happens, it's a match! The book writes us as much as we write the book, the dream builds us as much as we build the dream.

Create a Personal Vision

Whether you chose the dream, it chose you, or you found each other by chance through perfect timing, it is now important to review and gain clarity on the dream. This you can do by creating a personal vision statement. It is important to come to terms with what you believe you want from your dream and what the dream expects from you. Knowing the guidelines you wish to give the dream, and having insight into your hopes for the dream, as well as its outcome, is essential.

If you are having difficulty creating a vision statement for your dream, it may be a good idea to work on writing it down for yourself now. Try the journaling technique described in *Appendix 1*. You will be giving your dream a voice and yourself a voice as well. It helps to connect deeply and align the dream to you, (its creator, parent, instrument or however you wish to think of yourself) understanding that to some extent the dream has its own life or destiny, the final outcome of which is the mystery that has yet to unfold. Regardless of how you may be able to control its development, it is still a good idea to have clarity on your overall intent, a basic philosophy or a commitment to a number of ideas which will help the dream become a reality. In this way you give the dream a strong backbone, as it lives through its fragile first stages.

WISDOM 3

Who Is In the Dream and Who Is Not?

A little group of wise hearts is better than a wilderness of fools.
JOHN RUSKIN

Does Your Dream Have a Vision Carrier?

Although it is not by any means a *given,* you may be fortunate to have active "vision carriers" in your life; at least one other person, or a friendship circle which you can entrust with your dream and which will hold the vision with you. That is not to say that a vision carrier creates the dream with you, or necessarily shares in your dream (although this can be true when community or a circle builds on a dream and works together).

A vision carrier will steadfastly remain the keeper of your dream fire. Once entrusted with the dream, this friend becomes the guardian of the plan, willing to carry the dream when the dreamer cannot. And when she loses faith or sight of her goal, when she gets derailed from her purpose or enters a cycle of self-doubt or poor luck, it is often her vision carrier who will keep the dream spark alive.

A dream cannot grow in good health in the vacuum of your own mind. It needs to be nurtured with words of encouragement by someone who cares deeply. This individual is the ideal sounding board for the plan and can accompany you through the dry run of the dream, step by step. Some vision carriers show themselves early on in the dream, others come forward later. You may be surprised who can surface at a most crucial juncture, just when it really counts.

And when you become discouraged with the dream, and you hear yourself saying, "I'm blocked," or "What's the use of continuing?" that is when a vision carrier will remind you of the original dream, and will mirror it back to you. A vision carrier will also show you a reflection of your future self and where this future self hopes to be going.

Donna and Jim are friends of mine who work as a team to produce exquisitely detailed wildlife woodcarvings. Touching the wingspan of one of Jim's birds in progress is like caressing a velvet sculpture. When Jim was in the Canadian Armed Forces, he developed his carving by producing made-to-order crests for his associates. After their children were grown, the couple took a daring risk. Jim forfeited income security to devote himself to carving full time. His goal: to completely commit to his craft and, in the years he had to give to it, become the best he could be.

"That's the trip for me," I've heard him say several times, "to develop my skills to the point where I constantly stretch myself, until I create the best work I am capable of. And if someone responds to one of my pieces, so that after they have gone home, it keeps coming back to their mind so that they really wish they could purchase it, that's when I'm pleased. That's when I've accomplished what I set out to do."

Donna is equally as involved in Jim's work. They collect the bass wood together and prep it for carving. Together they set up and attend the numerous shows each year, the highlight of which is the annual Muskoka Autumn Studio Tour. Donna's hard work remains as crucial to the business as Jim's skill. After a mountain of shavings, Donna is still Jim's vision carrier.

Dreams can indeed be manifested without a significant vision carrier, simply by the combined energies of your own inner turtle and hare; Hare holding the vision, and Turtle carrying the dream on its strong back. Two people can dialogue and support each other through the entire journey and together they will get there. Other dream journeys need to be completed alone, because in order to honour who you are, that is what you may need to do. Such a journey may feel much like a Native American vision quest, it is the same on an inner level, without the customary ritual and physical preparations.

If, however, you wish that you had a vision carrier but you believe that you will not, perhaps you can contemplate this. Each of us can bring a vision carrier to our dream, even if that person is no longer physically present in our life. The memory of someone who really understood you, authenticated who you really are, and who supported your ideas in the past can help sustain your spirit. A distant friend or family member can convey as much to you over the telephone as anyone in close proximity. A vision carrier can be many things to many people. I believe I have a Guardian Angel who whispers guidance to me in my night dreams or day thoughts and who cradles the dream for me in my prayers.

Does Your Dream Need a Partner?

Just as turtles and hares may seem "destined" to marry, so also do they appear to be equally attracted to one another as business partners. If this is done prematurely, without some careful consideration of what each brings to the dream in terms of abilities, temperament and commitment, turtles and hares may find themselves frustrated when their hands are tied because of a poorly set-out partnership agreement.

On the positive side, the fable also demonstrates that although they are instinctually opposite in temperament and make natural opponents and sparring partners, they also have much to teach one another should they choose to collaborate. This interesting difference often creates an interplay of positive and negative exchanges that work both for and against most partnership and team scenarios. Turtles and hares continue to challenge and stimulate one another creatively in business and personal relationships of all sorts.

When spouses also become business partners, not all of these relationships work as compatibly as our friends Jim and Donna. And although some vision carriers also make great business parters, there are couples who wouldn't dream of working together. The advantages and dangers are clear. Trust has been established, along with an intimacy which may help in fighting through the roadblocks as they arise or may place extra strain on the relationship. Partnership may not be wise for some couples, particularly if one partner has stong needs for control in the relationship.

Partnerships between friends are even more fragile. Fearful of offending the other, or worse, losing the friendship, there is a reluctance to deal with issues as they arise. The reality is that most often the friendship does shift, once a partnership is formed. Sadly the relationship is often permanently damaged by it. What begins with naive enthusiasm, ends in wounded feelings.

Before you consider asking someone to be your partner, talk to him in terms of being either a vision carrier or mentor for you. Notice how he responds to your goals. Give yourselves time for lots of discussion to understand the perceptions the other person holds. If he suggests a partnership and you are not ready or certain, tell him that in all fairness to him, you need to think about whether any partnership is right for you, in light of what you know about yourself and your long-range goals. If you are pressed or questioned further, so that you are compelled to justify yourself, then that in itself is information for you. And if you unintentionally do offend, better now then later.

In a good partnership, each partner ideally needs to have a high estimation of the other's opinions, input and abilities. You need a partner who respects what you have to offer. If you have any doubt in this area, think again.

Subtle warning signals to watch for are:

One partner demonstrates a kind of arrogance or superiority. Hares can have inflated notions about themselves and their creativity. Turtles may feel very smug about their reasoning or time management skills. Warning Signal: "You should know that I have to be inspired to work. It's not like what you do!"

One partner makes shaming comments about the other's lack of expertise in an area, even though the comments are laced with humour. Turtles and hares are often secretly critical of one another. Warning Signal: "You've always been a little bit of a dipstick when it comes to numbers!"

One partner makes shaming comments about their own lack of expertise in an area, so that the other feels a need to continually bolster their ego. Secure hares and turtles don't feel slow or foolish. When one partner feels inferior to the other in any one area, this will likely hurt the partnership. Warning Signal: "I'm not talented like you, maybe you don't really need me."

One partner appears very influenced or dominated by the opinions of their spouse or another member of the family. A hare in partnership with a turtle may discover that power struggles with the ideas held by the turtle's hare-mate interfere more with the relationship than anything else. Watch for the "invisible" partners you may be acquiring. Warning Signal: "Oh, I don't know what to say about that, I'll have to see what _____ thinks."

One partner appears to have a pattern of same-gender or opposite-gender difficulties in their relationships — and you are this gender. Past or current power struggles between a partner and a strong male or female family figure are a clue and indicator for helping you assess how the partnership may go potentially. Warning Signal: "My father can still push all my buttons. When he starts criticizing me, it makes me feel thirteen all over again."

One partner is struggling with family versus career conflicts. Is there another hare at home, needing more attention than your partner might be able to give, or a turtle at home with set ideas about work versus family life? Warning Signal: "I'm not sure about whether I'm willing to travel until the kids are in grade school."

One partner shows strong signs of an addiction to a substance or behaviour. Or is still in early recovery. At first we choose to see only the positive qualities our partners bring to the relationship. See whether you or your partner are evading a potential problem area. If so, take the blinders off now. Warning Signal: "I'm working too many hours. I've got to go home and unwind with a few drinks."

One partner has unrealistic expectations either of the partnership or of the dream. This is more likely to happen to hares than turtles. When two hares enter into partnership, watch out! Warning Signal: "If we work hard for two years, we'll be on our way to the first million. It should be smooth sailing from there on!"

Your partner's lifestyle shows that some of his very basic values are not aligned with yours. Hares and turtles need to understand their essential differences in basic values. Look carefully at outlooks involving money, family, spirituality, security, to assess compatibility. Warning Signal: "Don't expect me to give up my ski trips to Aspen. I'm not willing to live on a shoestring just to get this project off the ground."

When a partnership *does* work, it is a shared journey that has all the elements of camaraderie, collaboration, respect, fun, creative satisfaction and financial reward.

When a partnership *doesn't* work, it becomes a painful enmeshment, which constrains the personal and creative growth of both individuals. It is, however, a learning experience from the viewpoint that unsuccessful affiliations are rarely caused solely by one individual. Clearly, it seemed like a good plan at the onset, but on some level we are now challenged to *own* our own actions and reactions in the process. For whatever conscious or unconscious reasons we were first attracted to seek out such an arrangement, partnerships can trigger our most basic core beliefs and issues. Making a challenging partnership work, or coming to peace with leaving behind a difficult and destructive partnership, can be a valuable lesson in completing unfinished business from our earliest years. And when all is said and done, we may have needed to discover that business partnerships were simply not for us in the first place.

Does Your Dream Need a Mentor

Although mentors and vision carriers may be one and the same person, it is not usual. More often vision carriers are individuals found in your personal life, mentors are sought through work or community involvement. My little *Oxford* describes a mentor as an "adviser or counsellor." However, to my mind, a mentor feels like much more than that.

The importance of a mentor to your dream cannot be underestimated. Actively or passively, nearby or from a distance, a mentor becomes a visible role model and may be a key player in opening an important first door.

From my earliest writing days, I wished for a mentor in publishing, an individual with influence who would recognize my potential and invest some energy nurturing it. With the publication of *Mad about Muffins*, I became known as "the muffin lady" in book and media circles. This, however, did little to help along my now finished manuscript on stepfamilies entitled, *Love in the Blended Family*. With several rejection letters on file, what was I to do?

Good timing, however, brought a well-known book publisher to our local library for a lively lecture on his outstanding career. I knew that he had been a maverick, bringing in fresh young writers to the business and having a wonderfully unique promoting style in a then conservative industry. If the middle-aged president of a well-established Canadian publishing firm could stand on a major Toronto intersection in a Roman toga to promote one of his authors, then this was the dynamic hare I wanted to be associated with. Mentors usually choose their proteges. This gentleman did not know that I needed and aimed to make myself visible to him!

To introduce myself to him at the lecture, and to convince him to take an interest in my manuscript, was the only "plan" I had. With that thought, I arrived well in advance to acquire front row seating. Dressed as if prepared for a Johnny Carson interview, I merged with the many faces who had come to hear about his dream. During a brief question and answer period after his talk, I spoke up in order to establish eye contact. The audience applauded, the crowd dispersed and, to my dismay, he disappeared. Horrified, I visualized my chance slipping away forever and, without time for forethought, I made a most brazen move.

I stood in an alcove, just outside the hall, pretending to be in conversation on the pay phone, while I waited for him to appear. As the publisher approached the outside doors, I timed my exit so that I was directly behind him. He was compelled to hold the door for me. I thanked him and he smiled in acknowledgement as we entered the parking area. Had he recognized me from my earlier question? Perhaps. My opportunity, finally!

In the very few minutes it took to walk together to our cars, I had blurted out a short biography, as well as a verbal proposal for *Love in the Blended Family* and its merits. As we said goodbye, he stopped momentarily, looked at me with a somewhat bemused expression and simply said, "You would be good on television, you know. Send me the manuscript and I'll pass it along to my readers." I was overjoyed! There was no doubt in my mind that he had recognized the hungry look of aspiration in my eyes, had even seen through "the sales job," but it didn't matter.

Fate was, however, not on my side. At the time of our first meeting, he was completing the process of selling his firm, and although he expressed the wish that he would have liked to accept my book, he was unable to make me a publishing offer. During this period he continued his efforts to create a positive connection for me. It was his letter to me, however, in which he told me that there was no question in his mind that I would become successful that most encouraged me. I was able to draw the support I had hoped to receive from a mentor. Eventually, I sold the manuscript to another fine publishing firm.

That his favourable impression of me would stay with me is something this book publisher had little idea of. Nor did he know that I reread his letter numerous times, whenever I had setbacks with the dream. As a silent mentor, this man has been in the dream all along.

When Your Dream Is Not Supported

Owl wisdom also means knowing who cannot or is not willing to be in the dream. This awareness is frequently there long before we allow ourselves to bring it to consciousness or have the courage to act on it.

Following the plan may mean the recognition that a move away is necessary. When pressures and expectations are imposed by friends or family, and you find yourself at the continual affect of them, you may need to create a physical shift in order to put a period of time and distance between you. It is an effective way of psychologically freeing yourself up for a dream and a lifestyle that you choose, not one that is chosen for you. You may have a dream where you need to function in a completely different world, a world in which you are perceived in a fresh way and in which you can also behave differently. When "coming home" involves putting on the mask of another persona, the someone else that you are, whenever you enter the gates of your home town or your parents' kitchen, it may be time to make change. In the future, perhaps, when your new choices are solidly in place, it will be easier for you to set limits with unsympathetic individuals and maintain your equilibrium.

If "coming home" represents putting on that mask when you greet your mate in the hallway, then you are faced with a painful dilemma. Some of us can accept this in stride, while others are shattered by the awareness that they are not able or permitted to bring the totality of themselves to the relationship. For these individuals, the sad realization is this: A partner whom they care about deeply may physically be present in the dream, but is not emotionally present. It is the ultimate "wake-up call:" Is it time to let go? Does this person still belong in the dream?

"How did I get in this bad movie anyway?" my friend Jane asked me. "I thought he married me because I was creative and full of dreams. But always I have to justify what I'm doing and where I'm going. I had hoped that he would trust me and support my taking art courses now that the kids are in school but he calls it playing around and thinks I should grow up and get a *real* job. Why did he marry me in the first place if that's the kind of wife he wanted?"

Jane has discovered the wonderful world of art and wants to pursue it. She's not quite sure where the dream wants to take her, but a career in expressive art therapy excites her, and she plans to acquire some credentials. The rest is an all-too-familiar cliche: the new friends she has met in art courses, the husband bored with art (it's over his head, he says and he's not interested besides) and the mentor she eventually will meet.

The important decision for Jane is whether to follow her dream, despite her husband, or follow her dream without him in her life. In either case it feels very lonely. And since he cannot be a vision carrier for her, she is lucky to have good friends who are willing.

The most painful letting go comes when we realize that, overtly or covertly, we have dream saboteurs with us. This kind of sabotage is often rooted in a kind of negative love or self-protection, in which loved ones may not wish us to acquire the dream, for fear that the relationship will change or that they may be left behind. Sometimes we imagine that we have the support of a parent or friend, only to realize much later that what began quite innocently has grown into competitiveness or jealousy. This is often not consciously understood or seen. Family members do wish good things for us, but being human, they also wish it for themselves. It is easy to be a vision carrier when we are on the journey toward our own dream as well. Friendships and marriages have faltered when one individual stagnates in an unhappy cycle of events, while the other continues to move forward.

We have come to a juncture in the dream journey where we re-establish balance and re-evaluate, not only the dream but who is in the dream.

WISDOM 4

A Dream Is Fragile

I have spread my dreams under your feet.
Tread softly because you tread on my dreams.
W. B. YEATS

Unconfronted Fears

It began with a wish. Feeling and desire have gathered the energy around the wish. Now it is a strong dream. Our ego is longing for it. And on the heels of that desire, there is fear.

Fear is a trickster who confronts you early on to sabotage the dream before you barely have the opportunity to begin it. And if fear does not do you in then, it returns with yet more power later, when the plan and pace is well established and you still have hope and confidence. Finally, just as you begin to see that your dream actually has the potential to be realized, fear visits one last time to thwart it, despite tangible evidence to the contrary, evidence such as hard work and past successes.

I see fear as having three faces, much like the looming ghosts that visited Scrooge in the Charles Dickens' tale, *A Christmas Carol*. Fear sends us ghosts of the past, present and future.

When I have allowed fear to kill the dream in its infancy, the feeling of fear was invariably my fear of failure. Ghost would take me back to dwell on memories of "failures past." Sometimes I was strong enough to resist the negative effects of the vision, sometimes not. In those times I was able to resist this saboteur, a ghost visited once again, in the adolescent stage of my dream, just as my confidence and hopes were building. This time, the face of fear was invariably my fear of deserving happiness. Ghost had shown me what a productive and creative life could feel like. When I chose to succumb to the fear that it could not last, it did not. If the dream and I were able to survive this stage, the final sabotage was always my fear of success. Just as the dream was preparing to the enter the world full-grown and actualized, the third ghost unexpectantly appeared to show me a glimpse of my fearless "future self," the one who had achieved both happiness as well as her dream. And that was the most frightening vision of all.

When I finallly determined to overcome these fears, the process became an entirely separate experience in itself, much like a fairy tale, transforming me into a child hero in a novel about my own mythic dream journey. I felt as if I had embarked on a long and arduous quest and, once committed, there was no easy return. I entered a dense forest that was overgrown and thick, and I found myself enmeshed in brambles. The road had suddenly become much narrower and, separated for a time from my companions, I felt abandoned. I wished I could return to the safety of family, but they were too far removed to be of help to me now. It was a difficult and lonely period but the choice had been made and, besides, I longed to reach the kingdom on the other side. Others before me had returned transformed, telling me stories of a peaceful and wonderful place. With fear as my shadow, I trusted that it must be so and I continued.

Experienced by others, this dream journey, in which we confront the ghost fears of the past, is always a psycho-spiritual quest and a return back to one's authentic self. In recent years it has been known as the healing journey or return to "the child within," and the "road to recovery." The prize is a feeling of inner harmony and wholeness, the strength of a newly discovered sense of self-esteem and, with it, the full emergence of our creative and spiritual self.

A New Dream Needs Incubation

You become pregnant with hope when you embrace the potentiality of your new dream. At last, the idea will be born and the dream will become your child. New dreams cannot survive without some gentle handling and nurturing.

A new dream needs incubation in a dream nursery with loving caregivers in attendance. Dream nurseries are found everywhere: on a training farm for purebred race horses, in art studios, basement workshops, gymnasiums and home offices.

Too much or too little talk can kill your dream, just as smothering or neglecting an infant is damaging to its development. Too much talk can dilute and minimize the energy and enthusiasm required to launch a dream. This is especially true if you choose your "first ears" unwisely and share your ideas with individuals who, in the name of having your best interests at heart, mirror only potential blocks, skepticism, "buts" and "what-abouts" back at you.

Too little talk can deplete or starve a dream. Dreaming without sharing your thoughts at all or formulating a plan of action, places the dream in danger of becoming a fantasy.

Take a Decisive and Strong First Step

Owls know that the first steps in a dream plan must be taken decisively, with will and forethought. First steps can be potential dream killers. When taken too boldly or rashly, first steps are followed by a crash. Like a toddler learning to walk, the burst of energy that comes with all first steps, may propel you onto your behind.

Some Negative Experiences Become Important Lessons

Creative ideas are seeds which need our protection, for they can miscarry unintentionally. This happened to me when I sold a magazine editor on an article which was to be the basis for a new book. Thinking I would have the first book draft finished and in hand before the magazine issue was released, I submitted my article. But life intervened. Another author saw the article, formulated a similar book concept, and did it! I had placed the cart before the horse and made my new idea visible too soon. I realized too late that withholding the article until after the book's release, or at least until I had procured a contract, would have been smarter by far.

Although the book plan was sabotaged, it was an important lesson for my dream. I had to give some thought to this; if I indeed thought of my creative ideas as my "children," then why was I so careless as to send them out to play on the street? Did I really value my ideas so little, or was I like the old woman in the shoe, with so many ideas, I didn't quite know what to do with them all? It was a little of both.

After a number of experiences, I became aware that I was consistently coming up with good concepts, although they were often similar to those of other nonfiction writers. For example, several muffin cookbooks were written in the span of two years after mine. This encouraged me to believe in my ideas more, and so I needed less reassurance from my supporters. Eventually, I learned from my naivety and understood how to better protect my new dream ideas.

Along with those early experiences, in which I needed to affirm the value of my creative ideas, I also had to question my abilities as a writer. My first editor rejected the three page introduction I had written to *Mad About Muffins*. I agonized over three separate rewrites.

Finally she told me, "Don't worry, Angie, I'll write it. Lots of well-known authors have been helped by their editors." Seeing my complete frustration, she further attempted to console me with one last point; "Some of us can write, some of us can cook, and some of us can cook and also write. You're a cook, Angie."

This individual had no idea that her words had devastated me, that I secretly longed to be more than a writer of recipes. I had worked hard adding small informative anecdotes to each muffin recipe and they had all been deleted with her editor's pencil. It didn't occur to me to question her judgement. She was a professional after all, with years of editorial knowledge, and was completely devoted to her work. I had given my power away from lack of experience and confidence.

When I moved on from cookbook writing to self-help, it was a giant risk for me. Throughout the first draft of 200 pages, I consciously had to block out the small but sharp and persistent voice of my inner critic saying, "You're a cook, not a writer, Angie."

This was Trickster in action; that master of inner sabotage who played tricks with my mind by whispering self-defeating words into my ears. When this happens to you, shake yourself and recognize that you have tricked yourself into believing that you have not grown from your past experiences. The role of Trickster (also known as Coyote) is to teach us how to lighten up, to see ourself as a player in a drama we have created. Now stand back and have a good laugh — as well as a little compassion for your old self.

Each time I think about the writer who hid out in the phone booth, attempting to "trick" the famous publisher into being her mentor, I have to laugh at myself. I also feel very tender towards my former eager self; a woman who would put herself into a comic scenario in order to be noticed, to have that first door open for her. Trickster is not always harmful. He can think of tricks which, with the right timing, add a little magic to our dreams.

When negative encounters make you feel invisible, when rejections and comments made by others are difficult to bear, let them spur your growth rather than trip you up. You are bigger than your former self. The saboteur and trickster are usually no one else but yourself.

A New Dream Has Strength All Its Own

Despite early bruisings, our new dream must build itself a strong immune system and grow strong. But it may not all be left to us. Certain dreams are sometimes like very special infants and children; they appear to have all the odds stacked against them, but fight to live regardless, and end up thriving. In such instances, the gift we receive is the part we are asked to play in this dream's life.

Whether dreams choose us or simply find us by chance, we might think of this in terms of "destiny." I have come to believe that, in some kind of divine way, dreams are out there, seeking to make just the *right* connection with those individual who can bring them to fruition. This was not something I accepted blindly, nor was it an overnight revelation. I realized it far more gradually as a "knowing." My consciousness became aware that certain experiences in my life contained elements of synchronity (symbolically coincidental events), and which I now believe were simply "meant to be."

Whatever the reason, some of my dreams simply persisted, perhaps trying to find life through my willingness and ability to bring them out. And pretty soon, before my eyes, I witnessed with some amazement that a little dream had grown and was getting stronger, demanding even feisty. Perplexed and a little impatient, I awoke each day to find it pulling on my leg, wanting my attention every minute of the day. Its time had come. It had found its voice. It had grown into a young dream that talked, and although it had fought hard to grow and express itself, it still needed me to set boundaries for it, and to nurture it.

You may wonder whether or why your dream has chosen you. Perhaps you will never know. But more and more you suspect that it has, and the dawning realization and eventual acceptance of that, has caused the energy to shift. It has somehow become easier.

WISDOM 5

The Rewards, the Price and the Givens

The dream is short, repentance long.
JOHANN VON SCHILLER

Understand the Givens of the Dream

Any new dream causes us to feel insecure for a time because of the personal risks we may need to take and the hopes that are attached to the dream.

Turtles, who have decided to take a hare risk, might find it comforting to know that in risking there can still be stability, when they know and understand the givens. Givens are what you *can* count on, and once accepted, make achieving the dream less of a struggle. When you plan a dream, you also need to allow some leeway for the new givens which invariably enter the dream plan.

You need to know this:

You will make mistakes. Expecting perfection of yourself or a superhuman effort al the time is a mistake in itself. Mistakes are a natural part of growing with the dream process. Your expectation may be that your dream will move in a logical sequence from one step to the next. This is rarely happens. As we correct our mistakes, our dream plan often takes more of a backwards-forwards course, like the "Simon Says" game of our childhood. Let yourself make mistakes. Trade in the word "mistake" for "experience," and you will be far less frustrated.

You will have setbacks. Despite your best efforts, you can expect setbacks which just happen, cannot be anticipated and may have little to do with you personally, or your dream. My first publisher went into receivership just at the time when my muffin cookbook was newly released and selling well beyond my hopes.

You will have unexpected positive surprises. Although setbacks and mistakes create their own set of unexpected surprises, you will also be able to count on moments of "grace" when wonderful things come your way. These will have positive influences on your dream. However you choose to think of this, be it chance, synchronicity, divine timing or luck, you can expect some delightful surprises which affirm your dream, often just at times when you really need a small, but meaningful good thing to happen.

Your dream will have both positive and negative consequences. Try to evaluate the consequences in advance, making allowance for the unanticipated mistakes, setbacks and surprises. Experience is the best teacher in knowing what the consequences of a dream will be. Most importantly, we have to be willing to take responsiblity for them. Our head may well understand the personal sacrifices we believe we are willing to make, but living with them is much more difficult. The whole notion of suffering and personal sacrifice needs some contemplation. It need not only be viewed, as some do, as a necessary and unavoidable given. It may not *always* be a prerequisite to achieving a dream. In objectively assessing the price, this is a good time to talk with others who have walked a similar road.

We think that we need very little help in visualizing the rewards, but this also is not true. Often we idealize the dream and inflate the rewards. One needs to be clear on what we imagine the rewards to be; whether the rewards are meant to satisfy us in nontangible, inner ways; whether the goal is to create concrete or material rewards; or to be a balance of both. Experience and other dreamers have taught me that, in the long-term, it is always more satisfying to strive for a balance. Assessing the rewards in advance is also a part of your planning.

You will need to make room for the dream in your life. The promise and commitment you have made to the dream includes also one more often little understood factor — the tremendous "space" you first need to make in your life to accommodate the dream.

Think of your life as a balloon, quite full already with activities and people. When you add something to it, the balloon must expand to let in the extra energy. This may work well for a while as we are all resilient to a point. Add too much and the walls strain with tension. You need to let some energy out. And in order to create energy and time for a dream, you may discover that you have inadvertently squeezed something (or someone else) out of your life. Friendships have lapsed, leisure has been forgotten, your children have seen too little of you.

Rather than readjusting and letting go, others try to deal with the extra pressure to the detriment of their health and energy. Imagine the consequences in trying to contain the extra energy that a dream requires. As you try to maintain your relationships and activities just as they were before the dream, you may find that your body has now become the balloon and is communicating strong stress warnings to you in the symptoms you are experiencing.

Whether your dreams involve bringing more people, more things or more ideas into your life, take note that something may have to be displaced.

You will likely end up with a somewhat different dream than the one you started with. That is not to say that what began as a dream ends up as a disappointing compromise. If that is the case, then you need to either redefine the dream or let go of the old one in order to make room for a new dream. Because it is a journey, you and your dream will likely end up in a different place than first anticipated.

I enjoyed writing cookbooks, and promoting them was half the pleasure. My first ambition had been to host my own cooking show on television. I never tired of watching cooking celebrities, enjoying how they entertained and taught their audience. Later, my on-stage participation in food shows showed me what a tremendous amount of daily turtle energy was required to produce one short show. On a week-by-week basis, this seemed like a lot of plodding to me.

Your dream transforms you along with it. As people and events step into your dream, as you adjust to the demands and challenges of the dream, it comes as no surprise that what you thought you wanted at the beginning has changed. And when the dream is ultimately realized, you may find yourself in a different place.

The Game Plan and the Dream

The price and rewards are subject to how well you can play the game.

When we play a game, we must make an effort to understand its rules and be clear on its goals. The trick is to develop an excellent strategy, and to understand not only our fellow players, but their plans as well. Learning to play the game is a lesson in itself.

Similarly, I must be willing to play the game if I am to achieve my dream. The plans and strategies I come up with are my "game plan." For me, that means that I have to know certain things about the publishing industry: what publishers are looking for in their authors; how publishing boards work; and the business of promotion and book sales. To be successful, I have also had to understand that, as an author, I need to submit material persistently and cheerfully having several irons in the fire at all times. And that I need to count my blessings each time I am invited to present a book proposal.

Be Willing to Play

Some people can achieve their dreams without knowingly playing any game whatsoever and don't give much thought or interest to games, hidden agendas or strategies. Perhaps it is possible for us to achieve our dream more easily and to its fullest potential if we understand the game that needs to be played. The word "game" is used in the best sense of the word, without manipulation, detriment to oneself or others, and in the spirit of fun and cooperation.

What an advantage for you, if you know the game and are willing to become a player, despite the fact that you may make some blunders. To know who the key players are who make the game happen, and ultimately, to know enough to withdraw from the game if it becomes necessary, is also a skill that needs to be developed.

The bottom line is that as you are learning what the game plan is for your dream, you can also do it with complete integrity. If you like the idea of the dream, but you don't like what you believe you have to do to get the dream, then you have either the wrong dream or the wrong game plan. The feeling of integrity you have for your plan and your dream is the best barometer there is.

It takes time and patience to develop the skills that help you in your dream. We all have to work this through. You have to desire the dream on a deep level to get past the setbacks and disappointments. My feeling is that half of the setbacks we create for ourselves are because we do not fully understand the game in relation to the dream we have. Once you master that, the rewards will come with less effort, as fewer blocks stand in the way of your goals.

The Persona You Project Is Essential

My friend, Janice, could sell "ice to a polar bear." Her abilities make her versatile, both creatively and as a business person, as well as understanding how to "read" the whims and needs of her customers. Her company has wisely recognized this. A key executive has taken some time to instruct Janice on the workings of the business. In return, my friend tackles her career with total zeal and devotion, hoping that in time she will be rewarded with a well-deserved promotion.

To understand the story, one needs to know several crucial details: each pointing to a growing sense of unease. Janice knows how to play the game, but she doesn't always like it; her hare enjoys the freedom and versatility of sales, but she feels her role is altogether too confining. Janice is striving for a higher management position, but doesn't want to apply the conservative, turtle approach used by most of her leaders. Janice's mentor may reveal his hare from time to time in conversation, but in dress and behaviour he projects a strong image of a hard-working executive turtle; when this turtle does take a hare risk, he ensures that he backs the risk with a well-executed plan. Most significant however is that, although Janice enjoys her work and the game, she nostalgically remembers her student days when she practiced yoga, wore cowboy boots and ate more holistically and less on-the-run.

"I worked just as hard, it seemed, but it was a time when I felt most like me," she confided.

When You Resist the Game Plan

There is no question that my friend had adapted herself to the expectations of her company. Admittedly, she enjoyed aspects of her work, looked and functioned as a corporate professional, but for one small detail. Janice adored jewelry, stones and silver in particular. She enjoyed wearing her collection of rings, the favourite of which was a large green malachite she prominently placed on her index finger. And despite the occasional remark in the board room, the rings stayed, a symbol of the creative part of her former self that was free of the corporate game.

"They represent what I'm really about, and taking them off would feel like I were losing an essential part of my identity."

Later, Janice admitted that her resistance clearly pointed to a need to rethink her dream. Perhaps she had outgrown her former aspirations and was ready to shift to a new game plan which allowed for more expression of her creative potential.

What I recognized in my friend was my own past struggle with what I see now as a rebellious kind of hare energy that surfaced at the most surprising times, just when I was most trying to be a turtle.

When you're in the adolescent stage of your dream, it's not unusual to have feelings of rebellion emerge as you strive towards the dream. Adolescents are hares, learning to deal with discipline and responsibilities. They have a strong need for freedom to live life on their own terms. The fear is, that if they play the game by "house rules," they will lose the independent ground they have fought to claim along with their identity.

Educational institutions and corporations both trigger the old parent/adolescent conflict within us. In the academic world, student rebellion has come to be an acceptable, if not noble role to adopt. In the corporate world, it rarely works. When the little kid inside won't allow you to play the game all of the time, your need for freedom will surface in your private life. It is here you can re-establish your equilibrium if the "turtle demands" of your job have become too constrictive. If you allow your rebellious hare to surface inappropriately or too often at work, you will find it counterproductive to the dream. This is also true if your turtle rigidly digs its toes in, if your path has come to feel like a tiresome and difficult journey. Would it not be wiser to take pause under a restful tree to re-evaluate the game and the plan?

If the Game Makes You Angry, It Is an Old Issue

If you have figured out the game, even learned it, and you want the dream but the game angers you, then you need to be looking at what the game is triggering in you. The players may be different, but does the office lunch room feel as familiar to you as your school yard in grade school? Trying to make yourself understood in the boardroom may feel like the kitchen table where you fought to be heard next to your brothers. Your family of origin was the first game you learned. Unresolved issues you have carried with you sometimes keep you stuck in the rebellious adolescent stage.

Here are some clues which indicate you are still enmeshed in an it old childhood game.

- The approval or opinion of your mentor matters too much to you.
- You consistently find yourself in a power struggle with a similar type of person.
- You find that you are consistently justifying yourself.
- You have established a reputation in the office that you are beginning to resent: social worker, clown, busy beaver.

Keep Playing As You Find Your Dream

I grew up living behind a retail store and was taught by my mother how to sell at an early age. I did it well, but didn't like many of her rules. When I left university, I worked for short periods in numerous corporations with training programs. I came to realize that corporations have their own unique games. But I wasn't fond of the rules and somehow must have communicated this, as I was not considered management potential.

Some time later, my mother wished to retire. David and I bought her gift and toy store, moved to the small town of my childhood, and I found myself back in retail. I was no less responsible, but I pleased myself: allowing myself to needlepoint behind the counter, inviting customers who had become friends into the back room for tea, and watching daytime television during slow winter days. This felt great for a while until I knew this lifestyle was not the dream. I sold the business back to my mother.

I then had a family and became a writer. I enjoyed the creative freedom of writing, and loved being part of the publishing community. I thought that I could project any image I wished, but discovered soon enough, that the editorial world had its own unique expectations and game plan. I made errors in judgment, and it took time to find a comfortable "fit" with the image, my style of writing, and a responsive publisher. But I liked the game so much, I was determined to play it well.

When I turned forty, our family took a giant risk with a complete shift in lifestyle. David left years of commuting to his workplace in Toronto, and we moved into a hand-built log home on a piece of land in Muskoka, Canada. Our dream now included a writer's retreat for me, a less stressful work environment for David, and the proximity of water. As we settled in, we acquired the boat, cross-country skiis, and other country tools and toys, together with the large garden and some chickens. The first year was simply a "chop wood and carry water" time for David; a much needed sabbatical and opportunity to renew himself on many levels. By the following year, though summer maintenance work came easily, winter employment was scarce; an economic recession had impacted the country as families struggled everywhere.

We had arrived at a juncture where we were experiencing first hand, a need to look at the illusions we had carried with us to Muskoka, and see clearly the realities as they were now. We realized that if we hoped to stay in the area, it would require a more consistent financial input from me. Having written about the "givens" of the dream in a manuscript just months earlier, I was now being confronted with several.

You will likely end up with a somewhat different dream than the one you started with. This "given" proved true when I rented a tiny space to start *Angelika & Co.*, a personal growth book and gift store. In an effort to contribute, I had once again returned to my retailing roots. In my forty-fourth year, I chose for the first time to use my birth name, Angelika, and create a business which expressed those things I loved: books, music, multicultural treasures, symbolic arts and jewellery. It worked. And although I did not anticipate becoming a retailer in the journey, *Angelika & Co.* unquestionably filled a need, and has evolved since, to expand in areas of personal growth consulting and workshops. I am still writing and growing with the dream.

Veteran Life Players Know the Game Never Stops

For me, the insight was this. Nothing comes without its rules, lessons and cooperative compromises. No game and no dream can give you total freedom. Once you have chosen a dream, and have an understanding of the game within the dream, you are closer to anticipating the rewards and consequences. Is the game plan right for you?

Accepting the game plan means that you also accept the necessary rules which need to be applied in order to achieve the dream. And if you enter the game "consciously" and "with good intent" and play it well, there is essentially no loss of identity or integrity. You are doing what you have set out to do.

Your image, or persona emerges and becomes stronger as you gain experience in the game. And once you have established yourself, your hare can bend the rules enough so that it will not be counterproductive to the dream. In a sense, you will have gained an understanding as well as a level of mastery and you can continue to evolve as a life dreamer and planner.

WISDOM 6

The Importance of Discipline to a Dream

In dreams begins responsibility.
WILLIAM BUTLER YEATS

A New Meaning for an Old Word

Growing up, I learned that turtles knew how to exercise self-discipline and hares knew how to practice freedom. I also experienced first hand that when turtles and hares were frustrated, they knew very well how to administer discipline. Most of my life I have thought of discipline as some negative thing you either did to yourself, or to someone else. I associated the word with synonyms such as: command, control, power, punish, practice, train and obey.

As a result, I spent my life being triggered by issues around control and power, in one form or another. Relationships were a major catalyst for me; working through these issues showed me a great deal about how I was not balancing my male and female energy.

When I became a parent, life became even more complex as I confronted my own confusion about personal freedom and discipline. I continually longed for freedom, never quite managing to acquire it because enough discipline had been programmed into my thinking to prevent me from wholly taking it. Determined to figure it, and my attitudes out, I attended numerous seminars and workshops. Childhood core beliefs about "shoulds," along with all my long held inner desires came to the surface.

It was not until I attended a conference on creativity and renewal that I was given an entire new perspective. There I learned from a wise owl teacher that the word "discipline" originated from the root word "disciple." Her explanation brought me to a wonderful new understanding of what discipline meant to a dream. When I heard her speak, it was clear that she honoured and loved the word discipline. What she conveyed that day, changed me; it didn't create discipline in me overnight, but created the *desire* for discipline.

Although I cannot recall her words verbatum, the essence of what she expressed for me was this. To be a "disciple" of something you love means that in order to learn or have that which you desire, you not only need discipline but *want* it, for your body, mind and spirit. You allow the work, art, person, study or sport to teach or *discipline* you. Dedication and focused attention over time is required during this period of apprenticeship. If you enjoy what you are learning and doing, and you do it with consistent regularity and effort, you have, in the best sense of the word, acquired discipline. Once acquired, you will look forward to each growth phase as you continue to strive for improvement or excellence in whatever you have chosen.

You Cannot Take Discipline For Granted

Much more than an established routine, discipline requires true desire behind it to make it last. We must want to learn discipline and the rewards it offers. Only then can we willingly apply ourselves to trying to develop it. And once established, we must value the lesson and maintain vigilance over it. You can lose discipline much more quickly than it cost you to acquire it.

There have been many things I have had good intentions about but placed on the back burner until absolutely necessary: diet, exercise, cleaning closets and numerous other goals. It was through child care tasks, however, that I first learned how to apply discipline to my life.

When our son was born, I soon realized that this helpless child was now totally in my care, and I had better develop a routine around his needs. Thus, I wholeheartedly embraced daily discipline as I devoted myself to our first child. It was altogether exhausting and boring on some days, but nevertheless it proved to be one of the most productive periods of my life.

One Discipline Inspires Another

Because I had become organized in one area, it also freed up enough time for new possibilities in another. I became restless and so began to write. Developing discipline for the sake of my children had laid the foundation for my first book, *Mad about Muffins*.

I established a routine in which I tested four to five muffin recipes each morning for a period of months. Highly motivated to launch a one-of-a-kind cookbook that had not as yet been duplicated, I baked my way through 4000 muffins and two subsequent cookbooks. The discipline that my partner had learned with his first paper route and grass-cutting assignment had eluded me until now.

Having children had finally given me the flexible and creative structure I needed. I found that this life style allowed me to accomplish much more than I had been formerly able to do in a corporate climate. By the time our second child attended grade school, I rejoiced in the freedom of unstructured time once again. I could squander or utilize the day in whatever way I pleased, and because I was who I was (a born-and-bred hare from way back), it wasn't long before I had lost my precious discipline as well.

Retrieving Lost Discipline

The interesting thing about losing discipline is that even though you can recall having had it, down to describing the detailed routine of your former disciplined days, it now seems impossible to retrieve. Like a bad diet, you begin each day with the best intentions, and lose motivation by mid- afternoon.

A useful technique for restoring a sense of discipline back into your life is to take a first step by choosing one or two areas where you wish to develop discipline. If only one area comes to mind, that will do. Make the choice, fuel the desire, and begin.

If you cannot think of anything that you can visualize yourself becoming devoted to, then the best place to begin is with some form of body work that you like. Disciplines like Tai Chi and Yoga develop a great daily body practice because they also utilize the discipline of the mind. These studies involve a meditative element that help to quiet and focus both mind and body.

This is particularly important for hares who are continually leaping around and who need to come to a point of inner calm. Some hares cannot bring the mind to a still point through practices such as transcendental meditation. Other hares become agitated with any kind of slow-moving meditative practice and absolutely need the energy of a consistent pace. A good power walking program might be for them.

Turtles who need to get their energy moving might look at activities such as tennis, swimming or light aerobics, to bring their mind and body to a more energetic pace. They may require body work that has more "spurt" to it, however, this is totally an individual choice.

Create Small Realistic Goals

Whether you are trying to restore discipline or wish to develop it for the first time, try this: start by creating a small realistic goal for yourself. A simple ten minutes per day devoted to one discipline is the beginning foundation for a larger commitment later on. This will be a hard task to accept for those hares who want to leap ahead and accomplish a lot at the start.

My desire to write daily is one such area in which I hope to create a "daily writing practice." If I cannot maintain the discipline to write for ten minutes per day, how can I hope to build to my goal of two hours, rain or shine. I must develop, as one author described it, "the slow discipline of art," minute by minute, day by day, until I can work up to a level of writing that creates productive results.

Our beginnings are always painstakingly slow. And it's all turtle! It doesn't seem like much, that ten minutes. It's nothing and yet everything, *if* you can maintain it and build upon it.

Build the discipline with the first small goal of the dream.
If you can't, then all of your plans and dreams mean nothing.

I have been taught that the most effective way to acquire discipline first, when you feel you don't have it at all, is through the vehicle of the body. It is one of the first ways you will see the concrete evidence of discipline achieved. You will have a feeling of well-being as your obvious first effect.

When the mind is scattered or confused, it is much harder to focus and discipline. The body, however, will be much more willing to respond to discipline. Whether in body, mind or spirit, balance still remains an essential key.

Some ambitious turtles and hares in the corporate or business world accomplish a great deal just from sheer energy output. They come home fatigued, only to wind down or wind up again in unhealthy ways. Perhaps they overeat, smoke or drink from nervous energy or exhaustion. These individuals have developed their mind, but have lost the connection to their bodies. As my friend Denise commented, "Some of us have hare minds in big turtle bodies."

Other corporate turtles and hares have proudly incorporated fitness routines. They jog or play squash, all before 7 a.m. Yet they may be driven by their compulsion to overdo, and mental peace may elude them. These individuals have developed their bodies, but are otherwise not inwardly connected.

Our first goal must be to find a balance between our need to honour the body and those needs expressed to us by our soul. If we do not, our body may let us down with symptoms that lead to stress-related illnesses. The mind demands much from our bodies; body discipline, incorporating fresh air and movement can also rejuvinate the mind, bringing focus and clarity back to it. Once developed, a sense of body well-being and mental clarity can be extended to other areas, as we lose our use for self-defeating behaviour patterns and addictions.

I was determined to apply discipline in two areas of my life: Tai Chi (body) and my writing (mind). After the short Tai Chi program at the local recreation center, I was very pleased with myself when I reported to my teacher that I had maintained two weeks of Tai Chi practice, for ten minutes twice each day, as he had suggested.

"Tell me this in two months," he answered. "Then we can call it the beginnings of discipline. Do Tai Chi every day, regardless of how you are feeling, regardless of the day, regardless of your plans, and see if you don't feel good because at last you have disciplined your body."

Maintain Two Consistent Elements: Time and Place

When a body discipline, such as Tai Chi, is practiced at the same time of the day in the same calm and consistent surroundings, the body unconsciously becomes programmed to crave this discipline, just as one might need a cup of morning tea. It becomes attuned to the daily rhythm and practice of an automatic ritual that is maintained with relative ease.

This holds true for any other discipline needed to achieve your dream plan. The habit of going to the library to study, the workshop space and the Saturday morning time you have set aside for your stained glass art, all this contributes to the satisfaction of having discipline.

Despite what I know, despite all that I have put into practice in the past, I still constantly struggle with sustaining body discipline in my life. Tai Chi is still not a part of my daily body practice. I have the desire, often go in hare spurts, and try to be gentle with myself when I lapse. After all, if I spent the first half of my life rejecting discipline, can I not spend the last half of my life embracing it?

WISDOM 7

Bring the Dream into the Day-to-Day

When schemes are laid in advance, it is surprising
how often the circumstance fit in with them.
SIR WILLIAM OSLER

A Dream's Not a Dream If It Comes True by Friday

This expression was coined by Dave, the contractor, during the wish-wall experience. And it is true. Unless you win the lottery, few dreams are realized overnight. You may receive a fabulous windfall: an unexpected inheritance; your book reaches the bestseller list. However, long awaited or a surprise, the good fortune must still be incorporated into the larger picture (and dream) of your life. A dream which is achieved overnight is often only the manifestation of a part-dream. Underlying longings will still need to be resolved.

A dream takes time and patience to be realized. And in order to feel that one is always moving, the dream must be brought into the everyday world. It is of no use to cherish a dream with no tangible day-to-day involvement in the back of your mind. That is a fantasy, not a dream.

When Obstacles Intervene

In trying to align your dream with reality, obstacles may suddenly apear.

I had planned to write this book throughout the past winter, giving myself time to "play" in the summer. How is it then that I am writing on this marvelous July day instead of lying on the dock, eating fruit? Last January, life intervened and throwing up a substantial roadblock. But as obstacles are often our best teachers, I now understand that I needed a winter of introspection to help guide me to the dream that I am now beginning to realize.

Dream obstacles often occur when the dream has a mind of its own. It may want to take you somewhere, quite literally, that was not in your original plan. The unanticipated launch of *Angelika & Co.* is proof of this in my life. Sheer necessity or circumstances may suddenly alter your dream direction. Or you might choose to think of this as the voice of your "dream child" or your innermost intuition. Perhaps you need to listen. It may be guiding you from a wise place within. Remain open and be willing to readjust the plan if you feel the dream needs it.

Obstacles Are a Necessary Part of the Journey

Not all obstacles are self-sabotage, nor are they even negative. Realistically, day-to-day blocks are a part of life, regardless of the dream. Therefore, not all blocks can be connected to the dream. It would be foolish for me to become frustrated each time I run into an obstacle that keeps me from writing. That would mean that birthday parties, an emergency veterinarian visit, and making dinner, would all be viewed as unhappy distractions.

This is a fine opportunity to gain a new perspective on obstacles that interfere with the dream. Is it not possible to simply think of them as necessary parts of the journey, too? That is to say, living out the dream means experiencing the peak times together with the lows. Both small and large blocks, plus a whole range of feelings in between, make obstacles as much of our reality as the magic of the dream . Creatively and spiritually, this is sound logic. We struggle to maintain the integrity of the dream at the same time as we must also "live life."

"Living life" and maintaining the integrity of the dream also means that while we must keep our own personal dream vision in our mind's eye and heart, we must not forget about the joy that is to be gained in the spontanious living of the present moment. Are we not also inexorably interwoven in the dreams of those whom we love? And in that, there will always be some element of mystery and the unplanned.

Aligning Daily Decisions to the Dream Plan

The degree of satisfaction in our life, the degree by which we can hope to minimize obstacles, may largely depend on the solid plan we give the dream and how well we can align that plan with our day-to-day.

If your dream involves becoming more visible in creative circles, then it makes good sense to join related clubs and associations in which you can network and participate.

If your dream involves eventual travel or a condominium in the south, then it's a good idea to have a solid financial retirement plan mapped out.

Adults stuck in the *"when I"* syndrome (when I grow up, when I retire, when I have money, when I make it, when I lose weight) have difficulty aligning their activities to a dream. The dream is always beckoning from a distance.

Now is the time to question yourself on some basics.

Is my work aligned to the dream? If work is a large part of your dream, then are you moving in the right direction by working in a related area? Getting focused and being in a conducive work atmosphere does a lot to bring the dream into your day-to-day life. This is no less true when you freelance. The moment I created private office space for myself, I moved a step closer to the dream.

If you cannot find work in your dream area, then volunteer in that area. Many volunteer positions have turned into job opportunities. If, because of financial constraints, you cannot make a career change, then return to school part-time and study in the area of your dream. Many people find that they can tolerate work unrelated to the dream if it offers them the time or money to follow the dream in another way. For example, becoming a night apartment attendant so that you can write the first draft of your novel.

Is where I live compatible with the dream? Is the environment in which you find yourself a positive influence? You may essentially be a "country mouse," needing the natural space of the great outdoors to get closer to the dream.

David wanted to work independently in his own small business. A time-oriented turtle by nature, city stop-and-go traffic, drove him to daily frustration. And then, of course, there was his passion for small-lake fishing to consider. If he was to live his dream in a compatible setting, he would have to move out of the city.

Is my leisure and where I play planned into the dream? Travel is very important to some, as are yearly vacations. "We work hard and we play hard," is something I often hear. One couple I know make sure that they have at least two vacations each year, specifically to enjoy one another without the distractions of work, family or children. To that end, they are willing to make other smaller sacrifices. "We need that special time for the relationship because we're so busy otherwise," they say.

Their long-term retirement dream is to extend their stay to these vacation retreats for the entire winter. In the meantime, they regularly escape to their cottage on the lake. This couple knows how to relax; their plan includes healthy doses of holiday time together now, and they also have clarity on the kind of leisure they are about. Others may have a completely different concept of leisure.

Whether you plan camping vacations together, venture on a bicycle tour or collect gardening books in order to dream about your flower beds, it regenerates energy for the dream. Leisure put off, or sacrificed entirely, until a dream is achieved is regrettable. How can you bring this more into the daily life of your dream? It makes the journey so much more fun.

Two Plans to Implement in the Dream

The larger plan is the tip of the iceberg. Daily tasks make up the massive body of work under the surface.

There are two plans you need to think about for your dream:

A *large plan*, in which you think long-range. This is perhaps your one year, five year or ten year plan; the big dream picture you paint for yourself in all its detail. It is part of the self-talk and inner planning that you have been doing, as well as what you have heard yourself describing to your friends and family. They are key steps in making the dream happen. You need to engage both your inner turtle and hare for this. The hare will come up with the vision and inspiration — the turtle will contribute a practical and oganized overview.

A *daily task-oriented plan*, in which you think in terms of the here and now. As smaller, but well-planned steps, these are your daily dream tasks that are responsible for achieving the dream. You need to engage your inner turtle to accomplish the daily task plan.

A daily dream task plan is equally as important as having complete clarity on the overall dream. These are the many small, but necessary tasks which must be attended to if your dream is going to be realized. The advantage is that they keep you directional and "plugging," provide you with tangible proof that you are achieving your goal, and affirm your daily commitment to the dream. Discipline and motivation are positively reinforced and you have the reward of knowing that each day you move a small, but decided step closer to the dream.

Keep a Daily Task Dream Journal

It is a good idea to keep a task journal to help you prioritize and create dream task lists to help you work towards your goal. These lists are completed, later adjusted and added to, as you live the dream out, day by day.

You may wish to work on a daily dream task list at a later time. For more details, see *Appendix 3*. For now, contemplate on what you might need to include if you were to work out a daily dream task list.

Try to validate whether the tasks you believe the dream entails are realistic. You may have your own unique idea of what steps you need to take, and that is good. However, see if you cannot talk with several people who are at varying stages of a dream similar to yours. If they are already engaged in the kind of lifestyle or work that you dream about, you can perhaps ask them about their daily routine. While making allowance for the very personal perceptions of others, it still gives you the opportunity to see a realistic picture and perhaps offset later disillusionment. In doing so, it may also create an added bonus: an opportunity for help and advice from one of these individuals.

Create a list for tasks in other areas of your life. This might be a good time to consider taking a time management program or reading books which focus on this. Include all of the small chores you need to get done on a day-to-day basis, over and above your dream tasks. Try to prioritize these tasks so that you are able to delegate or delete the "not urgent/not important tasks," in order to make room for your dream tasks. When you are ready to do this exercise see *Appendix 3.*

Important Life Tasks Compete With Dream Tasks

In trying to achieve our goals we can often put many unimportant things on the back burner. Closets with clutter, unweeded gardens, are examples of details which vary in importance, depending on whose closet and whose garden. I have written to deadline, quite unhappily, with nagging thoughts about my lack of attention to nutrition or the sacrifice of a daily walk. I have learned that since these goals matter to me enough to bother me when I discard them, then they need to be included as goals in my dream task plan. Essentially, they are important to the dream.

It is not wise to achieve your dream at the expense of your peace of mind in other life areas.

Finally, (and this is the hard part) figure out how, and who, will manage all the left-over unimportant, but very real life tasks that need attending to. Once you know that you are not truly living your dream unless you have incorporated time each summer for canning spiced peaches, then you have a great plan, almost. It's a dreary last consideration, but who will take out the compost, arrange the car service calls and so on? You may need help with that endless "dirt cycle" — those countless jobs such as cleaning toilets, grocery shopping, and laundry, that are only as gratifying as the length of time they can be forgotten about. A reorganizational meeting may be in order to delegate this list. Whether this is negotiated, taken off your shoulders or you have decided to somehow work it in because that's just the way it is for you, it is still part of the plan and needs to be considered.

After you have put your dream tasks to paper, plan to accomplish two tasks each day. One from your dream task list, another from your life task list. Update and revise your lists on a regular basis.

This will help you see tangible evidence of the work you are doing toward your dream, as well as keeping afloat with life tasks. Although they may take a back seat to the dream, they cannot be ignored. This is also gratifying for those around you (especially turtles) who, although they may be well-wishers to your dream, have difficulty overlooking dirt and the "happy dream chaos" of the creative process.

Accomplishing this final point is not easy. Don't give the inner critics a voice if you do not always fulfill these task expectations. Be firm but gentle with yourself as you establish your new routine.

WISDOM 8

Keep the Dream in Perspective

The ant is knowing and wise,
but he doesn't know enough to take a vacation.
CLARENCE DAY

Do You Have the Dream Or Does It Have You?

At the beginning our dreams draws us in and absorbs us completely. With our new enthusiasm, we are able to focus and commit to the dream, willingly devoting our waking hours to it. This is not only necessary to launch the plan, but good for its early development. All first steps are best done boldly. Discipline and endurance, together with a steadfast belief in the dream's potential, keep you going.

But later you may find that what began with a passionate involvement has taken over your life and resulted in physical and emotional fatigue and feelings of disenchantment. Oppressed by long hours, telephone demands, stress pressures and the needs of family, the dream stays constantly in your thoughts. At the beginning you had a dream. Now it has you.

The danger is that dreams, which start out with us looking at expansive horizons, end up trapping us in an endless claustrophobic tunnel. If 75% of your energy is being channeled into one theme (power, love, attention, etc.), you are likely out of balance with your dream.

To avoid disillusionment and burn-out, you need to establish equilibrium, boundaries and control over the dream. Pace yourself so that the dream does not feel like a compulsion so narrow that there seems to be little else but you and the dream.

Does Your Dream Still Feel Expansive?

One sign that you are on course and in balance with your dream is that it still feels expansive, is allowing you to grow, making you "more than." Despite the narrow attention that a dream demands, balancing the dream is an art.

Any dream which feels like one large drain, or "energy leak," needs a re-evaluation in which you might ask yourself this:

Is the dream right for me? Fatigue is often a clue that you are not living the right dream or are badly out of balance.

Is the dream becoming a compulsion? You need to slow the pace and rethink your plan if you are expressing addictive behaviour with your dream.

If I only go this far in my dream, and no further, would this still have been a good journey for me? In other words, are there any regrets if what you now have *is* the dream?

This last point is important, and one that has often been expressed by other writers. The journey must be at least as satisfying, perhaps more so, than the destination. Some feel strongly that the journey is all there really is. Rather than awakening to realize that you feel isolated and have virtually stopped entertaining yourself or others, the dream has hopefully taken you into areas where it has created more challenge and an increased feeling of positive esteem and life purpose.

Is Your Horizon Still in Sight?

Your horizon must be in sight at all times. Your destination must feel within reach, given your life now, as it is today.

Although your dream should feel expansive, in that you have long-term or far-reaching goals, you don't want the dream so expansive that suddenly you feel yourself on a ship with no map. A dream with no boundaries, no plan and endless vistas to explore can be overwhelming. Better to know which country you intend to visit first.

On a ship's journey, the horizon recedes as the ship nears it. This creates a series of smaller journeys that continue as each horizon is reached. In your mind's eye, you hold a vision of your ultimate destination, while focusing on each horizon as it approaches. And so it can be with your ever-expansive dream.

That means that I give concentrated attention to each chapter of my book, understanding at the same time the overall format and long-term goal. This allows me to keep my dream in perspective as I create realistic and reachable goals, one journey at a time.

Map out a course for yourself with "smaller trips within the journey." Your dream at any point should be something that you can see sequential steps to. In that way, your destination is always within eyesight, always within reach.

The Light and Dark Face of Sacrifice

I was once taught that in order to get somewhere in this world, one must be willing to work very, very hard, at much personal sacrifice. Only in this way would I achieve my goals. That work and sacrifice were virtues which went hand in hand was a core belief that I accepted. Discipline and responsibility were words that went along with both work and sacrifice; creativity leisure, and play did not.

Some of the core beliefs I associated with sacrifice and the dream were:

- If I sacrifice, I will have earned the dream.
- A dream without sacrifice is not worth having.
- Sacrifice is the price you pay so that you appreciate the rewards more.
- The larger the sacrifice, the larger the rewards.
- Others will love/need/admire or _____ me more if I sacrifice.
- Sacrifice is always rewarded.

It is no surpise to me today, that I achieved so few of my dreams in earlier years. It just seemed too hard. The media further glorified this for me when I read profiles of individuals who had achieved star status in the arts or the stadium; dreams which had been achieved at the cost of tremendous personal sacrifice to self and family. The message was this: work hard enough, be willing to sacrifice and you *can* and *will* achieve anything. These beliefs proved to have a double edge for me: as a motivating influence which would inspire me to express my full potential, this occasionally worked. It also had an equally discouraging impact, as I feared I could never live up to such "heroic" tests of will and excellence.

Some time ago, I arrived at a major turning point where I realized that I strongly wished to alter these core beliefs I had around sacrifice. I did this with a simple shift in perception, replacing the word "sacrifice" with "choice." Having done this, the negatives which had once surrounded the word no longer impacted me in the same way. It was simply my "choice," to do whatever it was I needed to give, put aside or otherwise offer to the dream in terms of time, energy and commitment. After years of believing that motherhood, relationships, piano practice and my career would require continual sacrifice, it took one conversation with my friend Sonya to shift my perception, *instantly*. Sonya simply rejected the notion altogether. "I don't make sacrifices," she told me, "I make choices." What was immediately apparent to me at the time, and a key, in my radical adjustment in attitude, was that I was also very willing and ready to let go of my former belief system.

When We Give Ourselves Over to the Dream

There are athletes, artists, academics, political and social leaders who live the dream so much that they virtually become the dream. That is, they have essentially *become* disciples of their own vision — their very name is associated with their ideals. Driven by some inner longing that perhaps needs no description or rationale, it may be important simply to recognize this. To give oneself over to a dream with that level of devotion (sacrifice) can be a life chosen and lived to its utmost in productivity and potentiality. When accomplished in a way that is not destructive to oneself or others, it inspires similar dreams.

Sacrifice As True Surrender and Service

Sacrifice in its highest state is true surrender and service; when approached with humilty, courage and compassion, it is an act of pure love. Rather than considering it a "cross" or burden, we sacrifice by choice, willingly, for an ideal or for the betterment of others.

This sort of sacrifice draws little attention to itself and is not commonplace. It is recognized more by its deeds than its voice, and is spiritual in the manner in which it is offered.

We honour individuals such as Mother Teresa of Calcutta whose service to the poor and dying, the world has come to recognize. She has become a beautiful symbol of strength and compassion in action.

Smaller, but no less significant acts of love are demonstrated by men and women today as they acquire a new understanding of what this means. To set aside one's needs, genuinely, without resentment, sentimentality or drama, in consideration of another is "to make sacred" (and the true meaning of the word "sacrifice," as it is taught by all world religions). Whatever else we make of the word is individual, cultural or academic. It is good, now and again, to re-examine our beliefs about sacrifice as it relates to creativity and art, family, work, history, spirituality, life, our creativity and especially, the dream.

Does Pure Mean Poor?

Tom, who was a skilled cabinetmaker, dreamed of making a living at his craft. With his wife, Peggy, he bought a piece of land, built a log cabin, and together they studied books on organic farming. The plan would be to work the land and become self-sufficient. Peggy was equally inspired by his vision, made it her own, and was a wonderful partner in the dream. Her gardens were as functionally beautiful as some of his pieces.

Before they had children, their modest lifestyle worked well enough. The couple was not excessive or demanding in their needs. But in time, with the many things they wished to offer their children, the dream was becoming increasingly difficult to sustain financially.

Tom made a decision to focus less on the custom-made hutches and fine ornamentation he had come to be known for. Instead he began to devote longer hours to kitchen stools, chairs and cupboards until he had established himself as one of the most successful and prosperous cabinet makers in his area.

Twelve to fourteen hours per day, every day, this man now works diligently in his workshop. Interested in learning from such a successful turtle, I asked him how he managed to keep going, year after year. "I have to, it's my job," he answered matter of factly. "In the morning I come to the workshop, and I don't leave it until I've put in a full day."

Because this struck me as more drudgery than creativity, I probed a little on his attitudes about sustaining a sense of love for his craft. How did he view his creativity in all of this, and how did that mesh with the reality of his life?

It became clear as we spoke that on a day-to-day basis, creativity was no longer the strongest force in his life but rather an occasional luxury he allowed himself. "Do you believe that *pure is poor?*" I asked.

"That's a good way to put it," he answered.

Before I left his homestead, I took a close look for remnants of the original dream. I noticed hand-carved furniture that contained strong lines, much life and showed a wonderfully imaginative mind. His dream was still very present in these singular pieces.

As I was in a period of self-enquiry about my own creativity, the encounter had a deep and unsettling influence. I worked with the question "does pure mean poor" for some time afterwards. When I think about this couple I wonder where they are in their dream journey today. My feeling is that perhaps it is still unfolding with new plans yet to be laid.

WISDOM 9

Sustaining the Dream

Dreams are the touchstones of our characters.
HENTRY DAVID THOREAU

This is the "plodding" part of the dream journey where, if you have not fully engaged the strength of your inner turtle, now is the time to do that. What you are sustaining essentially is the plan which leads you to the dream, and the energy needed to stay in the race.

For primary turtles, sustaining a dream is, of course, much easier than for hares. Turtles, however, can become bogged down with the initial dream, unable to sustain the visionary enthusiasm that hares are so good at. Hares, in trying to sustain the plan are wise to seek the company of their turtle friends for advice and support.

All the previous wisdoms need to have been well-learned and must now be applied in order to sustain the dream.

What have you learned about yourself and the dream? If you are wavering or doubting your ability to ultimately reach the finish line of the dream, perhaps there is one lesson which has not fully been understood or applied.

What Is Your Achilles' Heel in the Dream?

We may have one area that becomes a harder lesson for us than any other; it seems to repeatedly show itself as a weakness. Like our Achilles' heel, this is the one area we trip over time and time again. But with an extra push of effort and will, we can manage to move through this stumbling block also.

My own Achilles' heel has been that of not fully integrating discipline into my life. I repeatedly find myself engaging in an ongoing power struggle between my intense desire for the dream and my tendency to run from it.

At first discipline was the enemy, reluctantly I would let it capture me. In becoming its prisoner, it would force me to finish the project or write the book. I always escaped with relief. Discipline persevered. Each time I lost a dream, becoming more nondirectional with each disappointment, discipline sat in the shadows, waiting — for my *willing* surrender. When I finally did, discipline became a teacher, not prison guard, and I, its eager student. My "Achilles heel" had much to teach me about self-control and will and what it means, direct my strong mind consciously in a productive way to bring about tangible results.

Looked at from another perspective, you might also think of your Achilles' heel as your vulnerable side which, once mastered, creates your very strength. Whereas you may have sailed through other lessons, this area represents the part of the dream you least liked, most feared or wished to avoid altogether.

- Which lesson represents my Achilles' heel?
- Does this lesson trigger a childhood or old core issue for me?
- Can my dream be achieved without this lesson?
- If not, am I really willing to learn this lesson?
- Who or what can help me with this lesson?

Overcoming the challenges this lesson brings, tests you on life's deepest level.

Breaks Regenerate Energy

We are not gerbils or workhorses, although some turtles believe they are. Many dreams have been achieved with little satisfaction in the end because a dreamer did not know how to take the kinds of breaks in the journey to regenerate her energy. Breaks that include chores that deplete energy don't count. Writing bills, dusting or any form of cleaning is taboo. The philosophy, "A change is as good as a rest," does not apply to the endless list of tasks that have piled up around you while you have been concentrating on the dream.

This point of view is, however, totally biased and personal because I loathe such tasks. It may well be that cleaning floors or washing the car relaxes or energizes you. If that is true for you, then consider it the break you need. My friend who wallpapers rooms whenever she needs to "get out of her head" can't believe that watching our chickens or making three pans of apple crisp is better than meditation for me. "Peel fifty apples in lovely long spirals, and slice them," I tell her. "It's a very calming experience. And the smell when they're baking takes me right back to roots."

Regenerative breaks can include mini-holidays or weekends away or be spaced throughout the day or evening. Obvious choices will come to mind as you contemplate what activities make you feel good. From reading light novels to gardening, to time out in the sauna, you need to be good to yourself and stay clear of rigid or compulsive behaviour.

Some of the most regenerative periods for me have been when I made a place and time in my life to nurture a daily spiritual practice. This I did through my most intensive writing phase. With the help of music, treasured books of poetry, prayer, inspirational readings and walks, I was able to remain hopeful and centered.

Sustaining May Mean a Plan Revised

Financial considerations around dreams can be a considerable source of worry as we struggle to maintain the dream. The plan may need to be revised as we create a safety net to meet financial needs, while keeping to the essence of the original dream, as much as is possible. The biggest hurdle in a plan revised is often our initial resistance, to the shift in perspective it requires. Once any new revision is implemented and adjusted to, we often find that the dream is still very present.

David's dream was to leave the city and its pressures for the simplicity of country life, a healthier line of work outdoors, as well as the opportunity to fish. His plan was to start a small one-man lawn maintenance business with occasional help from our teenage son, and to service summer cottage residents near, and around the lake. The fearless way in which he made the transition was astounding. It became clear shortly after our move that this dream was completely right for him.

With solid turtle values and methods, he patiently allowed time for his business to develop. He felled Christmas trees on cheerless November days, raked mounds of wet leaves for fall clean up and stuck to his plan. During his first two winters, he renovated, chopped firewood and had time to read, for the first time since he could remember.

When it came to sustaining his dream, however, David needed to come to terms with a shocking new insight. Financially, his sole income would not be able to maintain this lifestyle unless I chose to return to the work force, or he chose to expand his small company into a larger operation.

Because we had not anticipated the barren scarcity of winter employment, David and I had grossly miscalculated our ability to support a lifestyle in which we were both freelancing. One serious new consideration was the question of how to plan and set aside funds for college education for the children, as well as retirement security. These, and other concerns required some creative resourcefulness on our parts — a revised plan with an earnest new "shoe-string" approach.

We wondered, should we pull up stakes and return to our former life? It seemed premature. For David, it didn't make sense to go back to the very pressure he had chosen to leave behind. For me, although my writing would always create income, it seemed that I needed to acquire some added skills. Beginning a venture in retail, never occured to me, and so I decided to return to school for accreditation in substance abuse counselling. In revising the plan, I had taken a circuitous route. It did little to help me find the employment in Social Services that I had hoped; the benefits made themselves visible much later, when I established *Angelika & Co.* A deep interest and participation in workshops on story, myth, and men's and women's spirituality, along with my training in addictions counselling, had given me an understanding in the areas of personal growth, health and healing. In ways that I could not have foreseen, it contributed to my success in business.

Vision Carriers Make a Difference

Learning to sustain the dream brings us to a most vulnerable point in the journey. Vision carriers, or dreamer supporters, underestimate their importance in encouraging the dreamer through a stage when it's often "just plugging away" that will do. When, as in writing, it can only be completed by the dreamer, this feels tiring and lonely. To have vision carriers in your life who genuinely wish to hear about the dream, despite the fact that at this stage it is an "old song," is a blessing.

Those individuals, who are "well-wishers," are likewise important. It somehow feels like the cheering section of the game.

At the most crucial point of this book, I received a note from my daughter, who was vacationing with her aunt and grandparents. Having missed her for days and feeling dragged down by the rigid timetable I had set for myself, I received this.

> *Dear Mom,*
> *I miss you a lot. I hope you are getting your writing done. Remember I believe in you!*
> *Bye,*
> *Kate Clubb*
> *P.S. I love you a lot!*

It's vision carriers like Kate who help keep a dreamer believing. Don't underestimate the gift.

WISDOM 10

Get Back on Track
When the Dream Gets Derailed

Adversity has the effect of eliciting talents which, in prosperous circumstances, would have lain dormant.
HORACE

When the dream gets derailed, for whatever reason, it is a devastating experience. You may have been jolted off track without warning when a life event or trauma broke your journey. Perhaps you had already feared an impending disaster for some time, as smaller crises erupted and created set-backs for the plan and dream. Although major incidents can bring about derailment, it is important to understand that as long as the incident is perceived as major to you, regardless of how anyone else views this, it is enough to create the impact which causes the dream to become derailed.

Derailment is a form of letting go but is more a "forced" letting go, often feeling like a terrible mishap. Sometimes there's a cry of "not fair" when a dream gets derailed — always it is a test of your inner resiliency, ability and courage.

It is difficult to draw the line and distinguish between what is a physical, emotional or spiritual derailment; they are so interconnected. What may begin as an accident, soon creates an emotional reaction that is equally serious. What begins as an emotional conflict eventually affects the body as a variety of stress and illness symptoms surface. Perhaps once you learn to practice balance and self-control through the use of your mind, rather than reacting destructively, your mind can work towards rebuilding the plan to help you heal the dream. This is often difficult to do and requires infinite practice, patience and, above all, faith.

The derailments which follow need all of your energy to get back on track with a dream, a plan, a life.

A Physical Accident or Illness: We have all been stopped in our tracks at times by an accident or illness. For a dream, this can be a major setback as all of our attention must be redirected to cope with a temporary or chronic disability. Temporary illnesses test our patience and ability to work around the illness. For hares this may mean being willing to slow down to turtle pace until they are back in full swing.

If a full return to wellness is not possible, you are now faced with a rehabilitation process in which you must come to terms with how this will impact your dream and plan. The shock of a serious physical derailment can quickly move you into an emotional derailment, which is hard to get past. If that is the case, you need to give yourself time to come to terms with your new reality.

Counselling and the support of friends and family will help, of course. It is also possible that in some instances a physical derailment can be an unconscious form of self-sabatoge. This was suggested to me by a friend, a psychotherapist, who deals with the body/mind connection as it relates to illness. A physical derailment may be a way of letting go of the dream in order that conflicts between the dream, the plan, circumstances or relationships need not be dealt with.

However, physical derailments are often confronted with amazing will and courage by many. Rather than abandoning the dream entirely, some dreamers fight for the dream by revising it.

Depression: This feels like a deep emotional weariness, where a disillusionment and lack of joy has set in after years of sacrificing to the dream. When the rewards don't measure up to the expectation, when they fail to compensate, or are denied altogether, you may have progressively slipped into a depression. And although you did not do this intentionally, your life has come to an abrupt halt. No effort is made now, either to pursue the dream or stay with a plan. As immobility sets in, you feel yourself falling. Try as you might to pull yourself out, you remain in a stagnating cycle of depression.

Neither outside pressure nor good will from family and friends can fix this lonely cycle if you are in it. More often than not, you may find yourself refusing both invitations and assistance. You may feel some guilt, however, nothing matters.

If this describes you, then you need to know that depression is its own cycle: a personal "dark night of the soul," for you and the dream. To surrender for a time to depression is a phase that you perhaps need to go through. Consciously fighting your depression is another stage in the journey that may yet come. And although it feels as if you will never move away from the numbness and stagnation, one day the energy will shift, if only slightly, and you will *know* that you are ready to move on.

Some years ago, a wise woman, appropriately named Pearl, told me: "Sometimes you have to say no, and you shouldn't have to bare your soul for it. For a time, let yourself be like a lily pad. When it gets too much, just float along until something unfolds. Build up your resources and nurture yourself." This woman was talking about the need for privacy and retreat in order to work things out.

Healing depression and its related illnesses is a private experience that requires you to explore much more than can be touched upon here. For some, depression remains a battle that may never be completely won. For others, depression is experienced as a spiral down into transformation, a new purposeful direction, an affirmation of their inner strength and renewed faith in themselves, and the dream.

Addictions: Addictions can develop from the accumulated frustration of unmet needs and unmet expectations. As our output for the dream fails to reap the rewards we hope for, substances become the poor substitute. Often, people who struggle with addiction suffer in part from a kind of spiritual emptiness as their day-to-day has come to feel trite and meaningless. As a balanced perspective is lost, we look to stimulate what feels shut down and "lifeless." A craving builds and we turn to the senses to help our mood, energy level, libido, *anything* to feel good again, even momentarily.

If inwardly, you worry that an addiction may derail your dream, you have knowingly or unknowingly allowed a dependency to influence and dominate your life. As the addiction steals the energy from the dream and distracts you from focusing on the plan, a power struggle exists in your life — between you and your addiction.

At first, addictions create the illusion of feeding the dream energy. We "use" substances or our addictions to stimulate our lifestyle or work habits. Ultimately, however, they deplete, creating lack of balance, fatigue and obsessive thought patterns. Like a fire that is now out of control, addictions grow and engulf the original dream until we are left with its ashes and the "nightmare" of a habit which can also potentially destroy us. The habit of addiction eventually forces a crisis that derails the dream and brings us face to face with the choice of seeking recovery.

Childhood Recovery or Abuse Issues: Addictions are sometimes the coping mechanism we use to "numb out," and bury painful issues of the past. Choosing to enter recovery for addiction can inadvertently bring unresolved childhood issues to the fore as well. Rather than deal with unexpressed inner rage and grief, we choose the alternate way and perhaps shut down emotionally (the lesser pain). It becomes our armor from memories and confrontation, as we try to protect those whom we love, as well as those who caused us our pain. This may be one and the same individual.

In any dream, even if no addictive behaviour is present, old traumas frequently resurface and beg to be healed. Abuse and recovery issues surface as old fears and saboteurs just when you least expect them. The inclination is to bury or put off making peace with our past. We can often successfully distract ourselves for years, with our goals, our plans or our service to others, until some life phase or event triggers a deep core issue.

Derailment happens when people and events trigger old issues for us: a boss echoes an old parental message, "Try harder, it's not good enough." A client echoes a long-ago teacher message, "You're not creative." You witness your child being shamed, and it resonates to the buried shame within yourself.

My feeling is that childhood issues are healed, not over a year, but a lifetime. In confronting our past and reconnecting with our wounded inner child, we also rediscover the inner treasure of our selfhood: the creative source of the gifts we can bring back to the dream. Derailment may now be giving you an opportunity to embark on an active healing journey, which leaves your dream at a standstill for a time. You will reach a point later, when you can possibly continue both your dream journey and your recovery process.

Situational Crisis: All other dream derailments will likely fall into this last category. We must learn to accept that life is constantly in a state of flux, and that the dream and plan must somehow be able to flow and be sustained despite it all.

You can become derailed by people in power who stand in the way of your dream. They may have the authority to alter or sabotage the dream, and often are so wrapped up in their own agendas that they are unable to grasp what you and the dream are about. This may be the crisis which tests the degree in which you are willing to compromise the dream. Your belief in the dream will hopefully get you back on track when you confront those who oppose it, or place yourself and the dream in a more supportive environment.

A financial derailment, such as a recession, becomes a serious setback to a dream requiring a bottom-line cash flow in order to survive. Your past dealings and attitude towards money, in general creative resourcefulness, as well as the support that you can generate from other people, all become factors in your ability to keep your head above water now. Perhaps you have done everything right, and still find yourself derailed by simple bad timing or bad luck.

When You Can't Get Back on Track

You have accepted that you were derailed, and feel that you have made sense of the derailment. You have asked, "How could this have happened to me" and "Why did it?" But despite repeated attempts to re-engage the dream and plan, you can't get back on track. The dream is not able to spark the same enthusiasm as when you first started out. You remember the tremendous energy you gave to it in its beginning stages, and recognize that a similar burst will be required. But it seems altogether too much effort. You don't understand it entirely, but you have lost the motivation and discipline. And you are left wondering, "Now what?"

Go back and clarify your dream. It's time to go back and review your former *vision statement* once again to see whether this dream is for you. If so, rework each Wisdom and stage of the plan to see where the blocks are. Do one thing each day, something that is not too demanding, but is a small dream task you used to do, when you were activily engaged in the dream. If you are a writer, that means you can begin to stimulate the dream again by keeping a daily journal. Keep it playful and just for your eyes. It will get the juices flowing.

Associate with other dreamers. You need to be able to stimulate the inner desire and motivation for your dream. Consciously make an effort to seek out events and people where there is talk and excitement about goals, dreams and plans. It doesn't have to be in the same field as yours. For me, going to an art show can also be stimulating. Meet people who are at different, but positive levels of the dream journey. This will generate excitement within you, as you listen to the progress they are making.

Until you are back on track, don't seek out other dreamers who are derailed. This is not the time to feed the derailment or the fear of ever getting back on track. For a time, retreat from friends who are as discouraged as you are, or who dwell only on the blocks and the negatives. When you are back on track, you will have more reserves to help others overcome their discouragement.

Spend time with children who have dreams. Nothing is more motivating than to "catch" some of the spontaneous ability children have to wish, to fantasize and to dream. Begin to listen to the dreams of children: let them inspire your own. Watch with what determination children tackle their personal goals. Be in the cheering section as you watch their dreams unfold.

Read creative, inspirational and spiritual literature. Spirituality, meditation and contemplative literature can help to bring back the deeper meaning that the dream once held for you. To read about courage and perseverence by others who have walked a difficult dream path before you, is inspiring. Whether you see yourself as a poet, farmer or both, there are an abundance of books and inspirational tools to affirm that life is meant for sustaining the dream.

Become a mentor for someone else's dream. When we see ourselves mirrored in a less experienced dreamer, we can identify and relive that earlier time. To mentor another dreamer is a mutually satisfying experience when approached with the right attitude. To mentor a child is exhilarating.

If you feel any residual negativity or bitterness because of your derailment, don't seek to mentor at this time, as this will come through and potentially discourage. Whatever price you have paid can be shared in a way that will help the dreamer's plans and possibly avoid a similar derailment.

Don't Push the River

To be able to dream again after a period of shut down and stagnation generates a hopefulness and excitement that becomes an important turning point for the dream. It also feels precarious and unpredictable. However, you are willing once again to become the enthusiastic hare, leaping after dreams.

In your wisdom and foolishness both, you risk by re-engaging your active imagination, as well as your will, and taking that tremendous leap of faith so necessary for the dream and the plan. Some will likely call you "the fool," others will applaud you. And although the outcome is never guaranteed, you have realized one thing. The dream is a cycle, a creative process, and in that cycle the dream itself is living and organic.

Re-embarking on the dream journey after a derailment means a surrender of sorts, for you are tapping into an energy that will carry you along. The lesson to be learned is not to push the river as you also try to steer. Once learned, it is a fine balance. And once understood, it will give you a way of seeing and living that is exciting, as you move away from the past and become *more present* in the moment.

Let us honour the process.

WISDOM 11

When to Let Go
and Seeds for New Beginnings

Hope is the thing with feathers,
That perches in the soul,
And sings the tune without the words,
And never stops at all.
EMILY DICKINSON

Bottoming Out: When It's Not the Time To Let Go

Where once we were inspired by the dream, it now is witness to our tears; tears which are a metaphor for the washing away of our many illusions. The moment of surrender has arrived and it is time, finally, to let go of the dream.

In that moment, we also let go of months, perhaps years, of longings and goals we were attached to. We grieve for the loss of all that we held on to; we resolve to cut the tie with the dream that is past. Although tears may continue to flow, we feel an inward stirring. Within the grief there is now a feeling of relief. And in that personal turning poing, to our wonder, we discover — it is not yet time.

Many of us have faced such a crisis; in the moment we most wished to let go, we could not. When every reasonable logic told us to end it, we could not finally douse the last ember of our dream. Instead, we held on, yet more fiercely. And, with a second wind of commitment we could not have known was in us, we went on. It was a crucial turning point, one that incorporated the intense energy of all our final tries, as we made new promises to ourselves and restructured the plan on which we might rebuild the dream.

When We Resist Letting Go

Most of us have experienced a time when we have held on to an idea, dream or plan longer than was healthy or productive, for us and for those who shared in the dream. Unable to accept that it was necessary to let go, unable to abandon the dream, we often desperately looked to keep the dream at all costs. Any reason, any solution would do.

The price, of course, was this. Hanging on to a dream that you have outgrown keeps you stuck in a place where you cannot possibly be happy. Resisting the letting go only makes it harder and more painful later when you do.

If you have been forced to let go of a dream due to circumstances: a death, business failure or divorce, give yourself time and space to grieve. Be gentle with yourself as you let go of the hopes and expectations you had invested in the dream. Be strong as you surrender yourself to an unknown future that has yet to present itself to you. This is not a time where you need to know where the future lies. This is not the time to dwell on the past.

Now more than ever, become the "lily pad," and just float, without resisting the currents within and without. Trust in a power greater than yourself and remain open so that you are able to recognize and receive the small gifts of grace that will come your way as you begin to heal.

When You Feel Trapped

The dream has long since died, and you are "hanging on" for some very real and necessary reasons.
These reasons are individual and many:

- You cannot move on due to insufficient financial resources of your own.
- Despite what you know about the wisdom of taking children out of an unhappy situation, the timing is all wrong and you know that letting go would hurt them more.
- Even if you were to let go, you feel that you are without marketable skills and have nothing to go to.

- You are afraid of the negative reaction and consequences your letting go will create for yourself and others you care about.

The years have destroyed any self-esteem you once had. If you did let go, you have no idea how or where to begin again.

If you identify with one or several of these reasons, what you need most right now is a plan to help you let go, much more than a new dream. This is one of the few times when the plan comes before the dream.

Even if you think you cannot let go right now, in order to let go one day, you must first work on believing that if the timing were right, emotionally you would be ready and *could* let go; that it's not over for you yet, and there is a life you can still build (even though you have no idea what that will be right now); and even if you cannot make an immediate physical change now, you can develop and be moving with a "plan" for when you eventually are able to let go.

Although this might feel altogether manipulative or "wrong" to you, perhaps you have little choice. And in order to protect yourself, or others in the future, you may need to become a "smart" hare or turtle and let go methodically and quietly by laying the plans and then acting on them.

If you need an education in order to let go, then start now with one course. Whether a correspondence or a university course, this may be the first step for you if you really want to let go. And regardless of how you feel about yourself, you can do it. If it is a job you need in order to let go, then start part-time. If that's not available, then volunteer. You will begin to meet people who can help you move forward. It's better than staying in place, stuck.

You do not need the whole detailed plan now. Do not talk about your ideas with people who will encourage you to accept your present situation. Rather, talk with someone you trust who might see a direction for you if you cannot picture your abilities yourself. And when a good friend tells you, "I can see you learning computers, or working with children," believe them. Above all, have patience and hope in yourself and your future.

A Mother and Daughter Tale

If you are a parent who not only respects your child, but in all lovingness is willing to support the dreams of that child, then in my books you have a great deal of leeway to fumble in other less crucial areas.

Here is a woman, who understands what it means to believe in her daughter, and who knows how to sustain that belief, while at the same time can let go enough so the daughter can open her arms to the future.

The article was headlined, "Help Heather Reach Her Dream," and because of an instant gut response to the word "dream," I read on with interest. Heather had been accepted at a prestigious boarding school for dancers, and this article was making an appeal to the community for financial support. Determined to become a professional ballet dancer, her parents and teachers had been clear about Heather's dream for some time. She had also reached a point where, at last, her hard work and natural gifts were being recognized.

From the time her daughter had first declared her dream, her mother had become her vision carrier. "I have always considered myself a big pillow," she told me. "When Heather falls, she can land on me, I can absorb the shock."

Unlike the parent who might project her own ambition onto a child, Heather's mother understood that Heather must want the dream as much, if not more, than she did. This mother also had wisely realized that it was now time to let others help Heather. She must begin to stand back and allow new supporters, perhaps a mentor, to step in on Heather's behalf. "I haven't even thought about what I'm going to do with the extra time when Heather moves away. It will be hard to let go, but Heather has to move on and train with her other family."

This however, is not a reality as yet. Heather's mother has had very little success in eliciting the support she hoped for. And she often worries these days about whether she is perhaps "setting her daughter up" for a painful disappointment.

So far the dream is still thriving.

You Have the Dream, Now What?

You have the dream and it feels wonderful and also somewhat humbling, for you are also grateful to those who have supported the journey.

You can now take a rest. Be the hare or turtle who rests under the shade of the oak, knowing that this time is well earned and must be savoured. Some dreams, however, won't allow you to rest too long by sheer virtue of their high demand in energy and pace. And some dreamers won't allow themselves to experience the sweet taste of success, pushing on again too quickly to the next goal.

If you can, try to let this satisfying feeling stay with you and celebrate the dream long enough so that you can feel fully the rewards and all that you have been striving for. The dream has to come to its own fruition, and this phase of your journey brings you also to a question which may already be in your consciousness, now what?

For active dreamers the answer is always to keep dreaming. Many of us don't, however, know immediately what the direction of the next dream will be. My feeling is that, for now, this is not so very important.

If you believe in dreaming, and creativity altogether, then you will also have trust that a new dream will float your way when the timing is right. Wise turtles and hares know that they need to regenerate their energy to begin a fresh new cycle. Creativity has its own regenerative powers. The universe is a vast "wishing well" with enough dreams for us all and from which you can draw your next personal dream.

The first prerequisite for you is to acknowledge and believe in your own creative powers. The second is to return to your own inner child to draw on the trust you need to believe that new dreams will come your way. Begin by starting to pay attention to the small significant urgings within. Then, like young Sara, make wishes, many beautiful wishes.

Epilogue

I believe in the goodness of people. Each time a community rallies to a cry for help, I see tangible evidence of compassion and support. An entire country holds its breath when a baby is trapped in a well. And when thousands of volunteers gather to form a search party for a missing child, we anguish, each of us knowing this could as well have been our own son or daughter. Regardless of the cause, we respond individually and collectively to the need.

Let us, with that same passionate love, become vision carriers for our children. Is it not also important to support that which does not have an undertone of fear and sadness? Let us be reminded of what is at our doorstep; a child who awaits our belief and support. How wonderful to give it, and to receive the joy that comes with nurturing the young, the creative, and the hopeful.

It is time to take the time to support our children's dreams, to give freely of our love to those children who dream of dancing, building, singing, painting, writing, inventing and dreaming.

APPENDIX 1

Questions Turtles and Hares Need to Ask Themselves

Take some time and thought to do these exercises. Use your journal, or jot answers in the space provided. It is sometimes useful to have someone you trust also do this separately with you. Then compare your answers. Notice the discrepancies and similarities. And share the insight.

Place a check mark in the area of your life where you are expressing your turtle and hare.

	TURTLE	HARE
Mate		
Children		
Parents		
Siblings		
Friends		
Co-workers		
Employer		
Community		
Leisure		
Creativity		
Money		
Health		
Clothes		
Car		
Personal Image		
Professional Image		
Other		

Although you may feel predominantly more hare or turtle, you may likely have identified yourself as both types in some of the categories above. That means that out there in the world you are expressing both hare and turtle energy in your life. Does it feel right and good to you? Although you are in relationship with other turtles and hares, the hare and turtle are also an internal team inside of you. Do you feel them to be in balance? If not, you may wish to give some time to the following questions:

Which of the positive HARE qualities do I express?

Which of the negative HARE qualities do I express?

Which of the positive TURTLE qualities do I express?

Which of the negative TURTLE qualities do I express?

Am I content with that? And is that the real me?

In which areas am I a HARE or TURTLE and don't wish to be?

If I could, where would I most like to make immediate change?

Are others perceiving me as the opposite type to what I really feel I am? Who? And in what areas of my life?

Now you have clarity on where you need to make the changes in your life to feel more "authentically you," that is more turtle or hare in the areas where you wish, or need to be.

APPENDIX 2

Creating Your Dream Vision Statement

In this journaling technique you will be giving your dream a voice and yourself a voice as well.

Find a favourite relaxation tape, preferably a progressive visualization which includes body relaxation and pleasing meditation music. Do the relaxation exercise.

Opening your eyes, you will write (in point form if you like) what you believe your dream to be. Add as many details as you need to create a strong and clear image of *where you wish your dream to take you in the future*. Pay little attention to penmanship, grammar, etc., and try to write fairly quickly.

Do this now.

Your Voice: Where do I want to take the dream?

Once again, relax in your chair, rewind the cassette as you allow your mind to clear. Do the progressive relaxation exercise again. Open your eyes. This time you will write what you believe your dream wants to become. Add details to create a strong image of *where your dream wants to take you in the future.* Try to write quickly.

Do this now.

Your Dream's Voice: Where does the dream want to take me?

With two highlighter pens of different colours, note where you are aligned with the dream and where you are not. The conflict areas are the ones in which you can anticipate blocks or some inner work ahead. You may wish to incorporate working out these conflicts in your dream plan. This may mean that you need to be flexible in terms of giving the dream patience and time to manifest, particularly if some of the blocks bring up core issues for you.

Looking at the aligned areas, try and write one or several clear sentences that best express the mutual intention and commitment between you and your dream.

Do this now.

What is my dream vision statement?

APPENDIX 3

Creating a Dream Task List

To work out a daily dream task list:

1. Write down the many things you need to do to accomplish your dream, including the related but nevertheless important details. We commonly procrastinate on some of the less appealing jobs, but they must be incorporated into the plan. As a writer, I might begin by thinking about the following:

- Buy a tape recorder for lectures, thoughts, ideas.
- Put a publishing proposal together.
- Network with other writers.
- Clear one hour each day for writing.
- Organize my filing cabinet.
- Take a computer course.
- Research new ideas.
- Make time to attend my women's circle.
- Schedule in yoga.

Note anything you can think of.

Task List:

2. Prioritize your list by rewriting it in order of importance to you. Put aside your personal preferences and do it as objectively as possible. Your restructuring of your own list to create your action plan is very individual. You may wish to group it into tasks you enjoy and tasks you do not enjoy and then work on a reward plan, moving from one list to the other, to accomplish your goals. Or, you may choose as I did, to adjust your attitude to unappealing tasks, viewing them in the context of developing self-discipline (See Wisdom 6). Once I stopped thinking of discipline in negative terms, I also lost my resentment towards the less gratifying jobs.

Enjoyable Tasks   **Less Enjoyable Tasks**

3. Understand what your dream tasks are doing for the dream. Draw up two columns again. One column notes the task, the second describes how it helps the ultimate dream goal. This will give you insight into the pattern to follow in creating your plan in stages. You can now delete tasks which do little to help the dream and reshuffle the remaining tasks in order of importance. This "task" in itself may be difficult, you may need some helpful feedback. For now, make a simple list of what you believe the dream entails in terms of daily commitment.

Task   **What It Does For the Dream**

4. Validate your perception of step number 3. That is to say, research and validate whether the tasks you believe the dream needs are realistic. You may have your own unique idea of what steps you need to take, and that is good. However, try to talk with several people who are at varying stages of a dream similar to yours. Journal the feedback you have received from other dreamers and planners. If they already live the lifestyle or work you dream about, ask them about their daily routine.

Feedback

5. *Create a list for tasks in other areas of your life.* This includes all the small chores you need to do, over and above your dream tasks. Try to prioritize them so you can delegate or delete *not urgent/not important* tasks to make room for your dream tasks. This might be a good time to consider a time-management program.

Urgent Tasks   **Not Urgent**

6. Figure how and who will manage all the left-over but very real list tasks that need attending to. It is a dreary last consideration, but who will take out the compost? A family meeting may be necessary in order to delegate these tasks.

Task   **Who Will Do It?**

7. Plan to accomplish two tasks each day. One from your dream list, another from your daily life task list. Update and revise your lists on a regular basis in your journal. In that way, you will be able to see some tangible evidence of the work you are doing toward your dream, as well as keeping afloat with life tasks. Although they may take a back seat to the dream, they cannot be ignored. Accomplishing this is not easy. Don't allow the inner critics in if you do not always fulfil these task expectations. Be firm but gentle with yourself as you establish this routine.

Dream Task List   **Life Task List**

About the Author and Illustrator

Angelika Clubb is a writer and workshop facilitator who specializes in universal symbols, myth and the power of story. She is a graduate of the University of Western Ontario in English and German Literature and the University of Toronto and the Addiction Research Foundation in addictions coun-selling. Firther developmental studies in Jungian Psychology and Expressive and Symbolic Art have influenced her work.

Angelika Clubb is the author of *Mad about Muffins* and two other cookbooks and *Love in the Blended Family,* based on her research and personal experience as a second wife and stepmother. She now speaks on the challenges faced by today's stepfamilies, lifestyle and career issues, and self-defeating behaviour and thinking patterns. Angelika lives in Muskoka, Canada, with her family and is the owner of Angelika & Co., a personal growth book and gift store and creative consulting business.

Janet Stahle-Fraser is an artist-printmaker living in Muskoka, Ontario. Her background in philosophy has greatly influenced her art which is rooted in myth and expressed symbolically. Its inherent playfulness awakens our power to dream and invites the viewer to participate.

For Information on:

- Current workshop schedules for Wheel of Wisdom, Symbols as a Transformational Tool and Personal Myths and Stories.
- Wheel of Wisdom Cards — a goal setting and affirmation deck to give your dream a plan and your plan a dream.
- A complete mail-order catalogue of symbolic arts, gifts and books

Write to: Angelika & Co. Mail Order
             Box 125, Baysville, Ontario, Canada P0B 1A0